The Jewish Music Companion

Velvel Pasternak

D1608282

tara publications

Dedicated to
Harry Friedler
Our dear "Uncle Heshie"
Whose love for music
And especially Jewish music
Has been a shared interest in our lives

ISBN 1-928918-24-7

CONTENTS

FOREWORD

A number of scholarly books that document the broad historical overview of Jewish music are still available in print. Noted musicologists including Abraham Zvi Idelsohn, Eric Werner, Alfred Sendrey and Peter Gradenwitz have written extensively on the subject. For the interested laymen without a great deal of technical music knowledge however, these works often prove to be difficult reading. This *Companion* is dedicated to bringing topics representing the broad panorama of Jewish music to the public at large. Four sections include an historical overview, artists who have contributed to Jewish music, annotated folksongs, and an appendix. Transcriptions of music with chords have been included as well as a CD with 14 selections representing the spectrum of Jewish folksongs.

VP

ACKNOWLEDGMENTS

Once again I am indebted to Barbara Cinamon, long-time friend and proofreader par excellence, for her painstaking corrections and valued suggestions; sincere appreciation to Goldie, my life's partner and long-time traveling companion, who not only allows me the freedom to create but also takes great pride in my determined effort to preserve the music of our people.

The following artists for the use of their recordings in the enclosed CD:
1. The Maxwell St. Klezmer Band— *Zol Zain Gelebt*
2. The Nitsane Binyamin Girls Choir— *Oifn Pripitchik*
3. Moshe Oysher—*Kol Nidre*
4. Avner Levy—*D'ror Yikra*
5. Flory Jagoda—*Adiyo Kerida*
6. Leon Lissek—*A Dudele*
7. Modzitz—*Simcho L'artsecho*
8. Moshe Koussevitsky—*Sheyibone Bes Hamikdosh*
9. Fran Avni—*Eretz Zavat Chalav Udvash*
10. The Zamir Chorale of Boston—*Hal'luyah*
11. The Gilgalim—*Ma Y'didut*
12. Lubavitch—*Ki Onu Amecho*
13. Sidor Belarsky—*Es Brent*
14. Michael Isaacson—*Instrumental Medley*

LIST OF MUSIC EXAMPLES

KEY TO TRANSLITERATION	
a	as in car
ai	as in sigh
e . é	as in fed or they
i	as in pin or me
o	as in form or boat
u	as in true
'	as in it
ch	as in Bach

CD SELECTIONS

1. ZOL ZAIN GELEBT   Klezmer
Recording: *The Joy of Klez*
2. OIFN PRIPITCHIK   Yiddish
Recording: *Most Beautiful Jewish Songs*
3. KOL NIDRE   Traditional
Recording: *Moshe Oysher*
4. D'ROR YIKRA   Oriental
Recording: *Sephardic Super Party*
5. ADIYO KERIDA   Ladino
Recording: *Kantikas Di Mi Nona*
6. A DUDELE   Yiddish
Recording: *The Best of Leon Lissek*
7. SIMCHO L'ARTSECHO   Hasidic
Recording: *Modzitzer Favorites*
8. SHEYIBONE BES HAMIKDOSH   Cantorial
Recording: *The Golden Age of Cantors*
9. ERETZ ZAVAT CHALAV UDVASH   Israeli
Recording: *Israel World Beat*
10. HAL'LUYAH   Lewandowski
Recording: *Zamir Chorale of Boston*
11. MA Y'DIDUT   Z'mirot
Recording: *The Z'mirot Sing-along*
12. KI ONU AMECHO   Hasidic
Recording: Songs of the *Lubavitcher Chassidim*
13. ES BRENT   Yiddish
Recording: *Songs of Gebirtig*
14. INSTRUMENTAL MEDLEY   Israeli
Recording: *The Israel Pops-Opening Night*

A Short, Historical Overview

SOURCES OF MUSIC IN THE BIBLE
A partial listing

The importance of music in the life of the Jewish people is found almost at the beginning of Genesis. There music is mentioned as being one of the three fundamental professions: that of the herdsman, of the metal forger, and of the musician. Music was looked upon as a necessity in every day life, enjoying equal rights with other professions, as a beautifying and enriching complement of human existence.

Genesis 4:21   "And his brother's name was Yuval: he was the father of all who handle the lyre and the pipe."

Genesis 31:27   ".......that I might have sent you away with mirth and with songs, with tabret and lyre?" The joyous escort mentioned here is an indication that already in the time of the patriarchs music accompanied the cheerful events of life.

Exodus 15:1 "Then sang Moses and the children of Israel this song to the Lord."

Exodus 15: 20, 21   "And Miriam the prophetess, the sister of Aaron, took a timbrel in her hand; and all the women followed her with trimbrels and with dancing." Here for the first time we find an instrumental accompaniment to a song.

Exodus 19:13, 16:19, 20:15   "And it came to pass.....and the voice of a shofar (horn) exceedingly loud and all the people that were in the crowd trembled." For the first time the instrument of awe is mentioned—the only instrument of the ancient Hebrews that is still in use today.

Exodus 28:33, 39:25,26 "And beneath upon the hem of it you shall make....and bells of gold between them round about."

Exodus 32:19   "And it came to pass as soon as he came near the camp that he saw the calf and the dancing....".

Numbers 10:2-10   "And the Lord spoke to Moses....make two trumpets of silver, of a whole piece shall you make them..." This is a direct commandment concerning the use of a musical instrument.

Numbers 10:8   "At that time the Lord separated the tribe of Levi to bear the ark of the covenant of the Lord to stand before the Lord to minister unto Him and to bless in His name to this day." This is the designation of the Levites in their fundamental role as the Temple singers.

Numbers 31:19   "Now therefore write this song and teach it to the children of Israel." From times immemorial the heroic tales of the people were transmitted orally from generation to generation.

Judges 5:2 The triumphal song of the prophetess Deborah.

Judges 11:34 Jephtha's daughter came to meet her returning father with timbrels and with dances.

Judges 21:21 At the Feast of the Lord "the daughters of Shiloh came out to dance in the dances."

I Samuel 19: 6,7; 21:12   The victorious David was received by the women of all the cities in Israel with "singing and dancing," "with timbrels, with joy, and with three-stringed instruments."

I Samuel 18:7; 29:5   "And the women sang one another in their play (in dancing) and said: Saul hath slain his thousands, and David his ten thousands."

I Samuel 10:5   "The band of prophets coming down from the high place with a psaltery, and a timbrel, and a pipe, and a harp, before them."

I Samuel 19:9   Each time Saul was plagued by fits of melancholy, David had to play for him

II Kings 3:15 The prophet Elisha needing the stimulus of music for his prophecy asked for a minstrel, and announced his prediction to the sounds of the *kinor*.

THE MUSICAL INSTRUMENTS OF THE TEMPLE

Halil- double pipe wind probably a single reed, a popular folk instrument used for rejoicing and for mourning ceremonies.

Hazoz'ra- trumpet, generally made of silver, blown by the priests in the sacrificial ceremony, in war and during royal coronations.

Kinor- a stringed instrument of the lyre family consisting of a body, two arms and a yoke. The *Kinor* became the chief instrument of the Second Temple orchestra. It had ten strings and was played with a plectrum, a small device used for plucking the strings.

M'nan'im-Most probabably a type of rattle.

M'tsiltayim- cymbals played by the Levites in the Temple

Nevel- A type of lyre differing in construction from the *kinor* by having a larger body and deeper tone. It had twelve strings and was played by plucking with the fingers. It was the second main instrument in the Temple orchestra.

Nevel Asor was perhaps a smaller *nevel* with ten strings.

Minim- presumably a stringed instrument and perhaps the lute.

Shalishim-cymbals or struck metal bowls.

Shofar-A ram's horn. In the Bible its function is that of a signaling instrument especially in war.

Tof- a shallow round frame drum frequently played by women (e.g. Miriam, the sister of Moses) and associated with the dance.

Ugav-still unclear. Perhaps it was a harp.

THE TEMPLE ORCHESTRA

The *Mishn*a gives the number of instruments employed in the Temple as follows:

Nevel—   Minimum of 2   maximum of 6
Kinor—   Minimum of 9   maximum—
Cymbal—1

Thus the total minimum required for the orchestra was 12. On twelve festival days during the year, two *Halil* were added. This was the actual composition of the Temple Orchestra toward the beginning of the Common Era.

Instruments pictured on ancient coins

THE TEMPLE CHORUS

In ancient Jewish life the predominant form of music was vocal. This grew out of the attitude that music should be a tool for the conveyance of ideas. Vocal music, by its intimate association with words, carried and interpreted thoughts and feelings, while instrumental music, according to Semitic-Oriental conception, served only in the secondary role of accompaniment or embellishment. In addition, the Talmud states, *D'kula alma ikar shira b'pe* (the chief form of music making is with the voice), the most natural of all instruments. The tendency towards superiority of vocal music could be seen in the regulation that although non-Levites were permitted as instrumentalists only Levites were permitted as singers.

Although there was no maximum size, the chorus required a minimum of twelve adult male Levites. The singers were admitted at the age of thirty after spending five years in training. They could serve for a maximum of twenty years until age fifty at which time, it was believed, the human voice began to decline.

Boys of the Levite tribe were permitted to participate in the choir in order to "add sweetness to the song." The Talmud tractate *Archin* 13:13, relates that the boys caused embarrassment to the adult singers because of their sweet voices and were nicknamed *tso'are* (pain causers) instead of *so'ade* (helpers). In his commentary, the biblical commentator Rashi points out that the adults could not equal the tone production of the youngsters. The *Mishna* in tractate *Yoma* records that one of the virtuoso singers, Hugros ben Levi, *haya yodea perek b'shir v'lo ro-tso l'lamed* (had learned some brilliant vocal tricks and refused to teach them to his colleagues). By pressing against the vocal chords while inserting the thumb into his mouth, he could produce tremolos in the oriental manner that would fascinate people. He kept his art a "secret," which brought on the scorn of the sages, and he was considered "wicked." Some others believed that Hugros ben Levi was "righteous" because his motive in keeping his art a secret served to prevent outsiders from learning and using this knowledge for pagan worship.

THE TEMPLE SERVICE

The priests recited a benediction, The Ten Commandments, the liturgical prayers: *Sh'ma Yisrael*, *EmesV'yatsiv*, *R'tsey* and *Birchat Kohanim* (the Priestly Benediction). They proceeded to the act of offerings. When the arrangements were complete, the *Magrepha* was sounded (the *Mishna* says that it was thrown). It produced a deafening sound so that "no voice could be heard above it." This was the signal for the Priests to enter the Temple and to prostrate themselves and for the Levites to begin the musical performance.

Two Priests immediately took their stand at the Altar and began to blow the trumpets-*teki'a*, *teru'a*, *teki'a* (the three standard *shofar* sounds) The Priests then approached Ben Arza, the cymbal player, and flanked him. At a given signal, Ben Arza sounded the cymbal and the Levites began to sing the Psalm of the Day. Whenever they finished a section, they stopped; the priests blew the trumpets once again and all the people prostrated themselves. The texts sung by the Levites were not only Psalms but also portions of the Pentateuch.

This description does not indicate whether the singers were accompanied by the instruments or if the choir and orchestra worked alternately. A short time after the destruction of the Temple the entire art of instrumental music fell into oblivion.

Instrumental music, according to Semitic-Oriental conception serves only as accompaniment and embellishment. The vocal singing, including the psalm singing and the Pentateuch as well as the recitation of the prayers, was retained and transplanted into the *bet haknesset* (the synagogue) an institution established long before the destruction of the Second Temple. The *Talmud Yerushalmi* (*Megila* 3:1) records that there were 480 synagogues in Jerusalem at the time of the conquest by the Romans.

The *Mishna* (*Taanit* 4:2) describes the institution of the *Anshe Ma'amad*, an organization of laymen, delegates of the people, established mainly for the purpose of transplanting the routine of

Temple liturgy in its authentic form to far off places. The country was divided into twenty-four sections, each delegating a representative to Jerusalem who would attend the Temple services twice a year for a period of one week. Back home again, these delegates would make sure that the rites, customs and melodies in their own synagogues were performed according to the traditions of the Temple.

THE SYNAGOGUE PRECENTOR

Long before the establishment of worship in Israel, ancient nations such as the Assyrians, Babylonians and Egyptians had developed an organized service with responsive prayers. During these prayers, the priest functioned as reader and precentor while the priestly choir, and occasionally the public, participated with responses. Jewish worship differed from that of the ancient nations in one important aspect. In the above mentioned nations, the priest acted as precentor while simultaneously offering sacrifices. He recited the prayers and was the only mediator between his people and God. In Judaism, however, through the influence of the prophets, the idea became prevalent that God is near to everybody and that everyone can approach Him. The relationship between God and Israel, as between father and children, entitled everyone to pray without priestly mediation. We see this relationship in Jewish liturgy by the use of the familiar form *Ata* (You) when addressing God during prayer.

Because the people did not have sufficient education to express their wishes, usually a prominent man, "one of the people" would serve as the intercessor. In ancient times such a spokesman was known as *mitpalel* (lit. lead oneself to pray). He became the intercessor of the people because he was recognized as one endowed with the rare power of praying. It is an interesting phenomenon of Judaism that, from the very beginning, these spokesmen were all men of the people.

15

Due to Greek influence, the rabbis became aware that singing had not only pure functional attributes but could also be beautiful. They soon began to choose precentors who were endowed with particularly fine voices. The passage in Proverbs 3:9, *Kabed et Hashem mehonecha* (Honor your Lord with your substance) was interpreted to mean that every possessor of a beautiful voice was obliged to lead in prayer. The *Mishna* also states that the word *hon* (substance or wealth) should be read *garon* (throat).

It was only a natural development that the office of precentor was gradually transferred from the priests to those chosen because of their vocal and musical abilities. The office of precentor became a position of honor which could only be filled by men of high moral character and reputation. Rabbi Judah ben-Illai (*Talmud Taanith* 16:a) gives the following description of the ideal precentor:

> He should be a learned man who has music in himself and is endowed with an agreeable voice, who is humble, has a pleasant appearance, is recognized by and popular with the community, is conversant with the Scriptures, able to preach a sermon, well versed in law and folklore, and who knows all the prayers by heart. He should also be poor and needy for then his prayers will come from his heart.

At a later stage the precentor was given two assistants called *tomchim* or *mesayim* (supporters) whose duty it was to remind him of the prayers and their tunes. The prayers and melodies were passed down orally until the seventh century when they were first allowed to be written. The two assistants, already mentioned in the third century, have been retained in synagogues services. In traditional synagogues, especially on the Day of Atonement and during Torah reading, two men stand by the *baal t'filoh* and the *baal kriya* (Torah reader).

In the decades following the completion of the Talmud, Jews suffered under Christian oppression in Palestine and from the Magi Caste in Babylonia. Many of their cultural centers were destroyed, and for a time the schools had to close their doors. The hardship of the times brought about great difficulties in the organization of worship and education and it was impossible to find precentors. The institution of the professional *shali'ach tsibur* (precentor) became necessary. Later he was called *chazan*, a term that had formerly described a secular official, an "overseer," but after the destruction of the Second Temple, it simply meant beadle. As the beadle was always present at the synagogue service, it was logical to introduce him to the office of the precentor. With time, he acquired professional knowledge and skill. Although unmarried men had not been permitted to serve as *chazan*, the difficulties of the time can be seen in the rulings of some eighth and ninth century scholars that youths of seventeen or eighteen, and in the case of emergency, even boys of thirteen were eligible for the office of *chazan*.

Of all the requirements, the possession of a sweet voice was considered the most essential. It was thought to be a heavenly gift given to inspire devotion. Good pronunciation and distinct articulation were considered essential; one who stammered or stuttered could not lead services. As an indication of reverence and humility in worship, the sages insisted that the precentor should stand on a lower level than the other worshippers. This conformed with Psalm 130:1, "Out of the depths I cry to Thee." Many synagogues retained the custom of having the precentor's platform lower than the floor of the synagogue. Only for the reading of the Scriptures was there a *bima* (an elevated platform) in the center of the synagogue.

The style of the ancient prayers continued until the sixth century when more intricate poetical forms known as *piyut* were introduced. The music for *piyut* required more talent than the simplistic melodies common until then. It was necessary for professional singers to devote themselves to the study and cultivation of the new texts and their melodies, a task that was impossible for the lay precentors. The position of professional precentor, or *chazan*, was therefore created because of ignorance on one hand, and the new artistic demands on the other. The professional however, even after he became the permanent *shaliach tsibur*, could not replace the precentor. The latter never completely disappeared from the synagogue. Throughout the Middle Ages, and in many places down to our own times, prominent men of high ethical standing, rabbis or laymen, functioned as *chazanim*. This was especially true on Yom Kippur and the Three Festivals, when many rabbis served as the *shaliach tsibur* during the closing *Neila* and *Hallel* services.

Along with the Psalms and part of the Jewish ritual, the early Christians transplanted the institution of the precentor from the synagogue into the church. The solo recitation of the precentor became the chief part of the church service. Similarly, the responsive form used in the Temple and synagogue was adopted by the church, especially short refrains such as *Amen, Halleluya, Hosanna, Ki l'olam chasdo*. The church singer was called *cantor, praecenter*, and *pronunciator psalmi*. Originally, there was also a *lektor* (reader) and the cantor (singer) in the church. As in the synagogue, an elevated stand was erected for the church *lektor* from which the scriptures were read. The precentor in the church, however, gradually gave way to the choir, and the choral song replaced the solo recitation. Thus, the precentor vanished completely in some churches, and in others his role was reduced to an insignificant function. In the synagogue, however, the precentor maintained his importance.

BIBLICAL CHANT

All reading and study of the Torah, and later of the Koran among Mohammedans, were done with a speech melody known as Cantillation. Among the Jews the *neumes* (signs) are known as *N'ginot, T'amim, T'ame Han'ginot, N'imoth* as well as accents and tropes. *N'ginoth*-from the word *nigun,* tune; *T'amim* from the word *taam* meaning sense (revealing the sense of the word); *N'imoth*-from the word *na'im* meaning sweet (adding sweetness to the words of the Torah). *N'imoth* has also been traced to the Greek word *neume* meaning musical sign.

The evolution of the synagogue musical tradition may be said to have taken place as follows:

1. First came the gradually shaped cantillation modes.
2. Out of these emerged the prayer modes-*Nusach Hatfila*
3. From the prayer modes came the traditional melodies e.g. *Kol Nidre*, etc.
4. Out of these foundations came the folk song, the art song and art music.

The first commandment to read the Torah in public places is found in Deuteronomy 31:11,12. Moses commanded Israel to read the Torah at a great convocation to be held every seven years on the Feast of Tabernacles when all Israel gathered in Jerusalem. In 444 BCE, when Israel returned from Babylonian captivity, Ezra read the Torah publicly, no doubt with melody, in one of the open squares in Jerusalem. Because the tradition to read the Torah with melody was considered sacred, it was guarded and perpetuated. The Torah readings continued in the traditional manner until the eighth century CE. At this time, a system of accents and their musical interpretation was instituted. The process was not independent, for the *neume* system employed by the Jews was fashioned after the Greek and Syriac systems of interpunction. The crude musical notation, which was being fashioned and perfected during the same period in the musical world at large, also influenced Jewish musical efforts in that direction.

Between the fifth and ninth centuries, the Catholic Church was codifying and perfecting Gregorian Chant. While the Christian musical world was devising a system of notation, the Jews were not idle. The Ben Asher family in Tiberias, Palestine, became interested in proper accentuation and systematic presentation. This activity culminated in the ninth century when Aaron ben Asher established the vocal punctuation in the Bible and created the first scroll with such punctuation.

Modern day musicologists agree with the early Church fathers who contend that both Greek Orthodox chant and Catholic Gregorian chant were derived from the Temple and synagogue of ancient Palestine. Music history illustrates that early art music was derived largely from the music of the Church. The conclusion from these historical facts is that ancient biblical chant served as at least one of the basic pillars of art music as we know it.

There is ample evidence of biblical chant as early as the second century A.D. by which time it was already an established custom. In the third century A.D., Rav interpreted the verse "And they read in the book, in the Law of God....and caused them to understand the reading" (Neh.8:8). as a reference to the *piske taamim* (the punctuation) by means of melodic cadences (*Megillah* 3A). Rabbi Akiva expressed his demand for daily study, also executed in chant, by the words, "Sing it every day, sing it every day. He who reads the Pentateuch without tune shows disregard for it and the vital value of its laws" (*Megillah* 32:B).

It was intentional that public biblical readings were instituted. However, only those books read in public were supplied with *taamim*, among them: Pentateuch, Prophets, Scroll of Esther, Lamentations, Ruth, Ecclesiastes, Song of Songs, Psalms, and Job (in some communities). Books not read in public were Proverbs, Ezra, Nehemiah, and Chronicles.

גַּרְשַׁיִם	סִלּוּק
אַזְלָא	אֶתְנָח, אַתְנַחְתָּא
פָּזֵר	טִפְחָא
תְּלִישָׁא גְדוֹלָה	סֶגוֹל, סֶגוֹלְתָּא
קַרְנֵי־פָרָה	שַׁלְשֶׁלֶת
מוּנַח לְנַרְמֵיהּ / מוּנַח	זָקֵף קָטֹן
מֵירְכָא	זָקֵף גָּדוֹל
מֵירְכָא כְפוּלָה / מַהְפָּךְ	רְבִיעַ
דַּרְגָּא	תְּבִיר
קַדְמָא	זַרְקָא
תְּלִישָׁא קְטַנָּה / יָרַח בֶּן־יוֹמוֹ	פַּשְׁטָא
פְּסִיק	יְתִיב
	גֶּרֶשׁ, גֵּרֵשׁ

Cantillation Signs

Earliest known notation of the Torah chant

RABBINIC ATTITUDE TOWARDS MUSIC

After the destruction of the Temple in Jerusalem, it seemed that music was doomed to be silenced forever within Judaism. Before the destruction, secular music was already considered a bad influence. Greek song, especially, was thought to be harmful. The spiritual leaders of Israel tried to fight against these influences by urging the people to sing only religious songs during their festive occasions. The rabbis challenged all singers:

> If you have a sweet voice, glorify God with the gift He bestowed upon you, chant the *Sh'ma*, and lead the people in prayer. Profane songs of love and lust are sufficient cause to destroy the world but religious songs save it. Whenever God hears Israel's song, He calls the heavenly host to listen.

Following the destruction, all instrumental music, even for religious purposes, was prohibited as a sign of national mourning. At the beginning of the third century, Abba Areka (Rav) stated, "an ear which listens to music (secular) shall be torn out." A generation later Rabba stated, "Music in a house must bring the house to destruction." His colleague, Rabbi Joseph, expressed the opinion that "if men sing and women respond, the result is licentiousness, but if women sing and men respond, the end is like a flame in hatcheled flax."

This attitude was not unique to the rabbis. By the beginning of the Common Era, Greek art and culture had degenerated to mere virtuosity, empty of any ideal. Music became a means to stimulate voluptuousness and was synonymous with licentiousness and obscenity. It was used primarily for carnal purposes at frivolous occasions. Christianity, like Judaism, fought the heathen music bitterly. Within a short time, no instrument was used in any Christian service. The strict order of the Church Fathers, that only unaccompanied voice would be allowed for the liturgy, is still observed in the Syriac, Jacobite, Nestorian and Greek churches into the 21st century.

In the synagogue, also, no instrument was used in the service until 1810 when the organ was introduced in the first Reform Temple in

Seesen, Germany. Unlike the Church, however, this prohibition in the synagogue had a national motive. Rabbincal leaders believed that no instrument should be used until the Temple was restored and Levites would again conduct the musical service. In addition, the playing of musical instruments on Sabbaths and festivals was regarded as a desecration, for it was possible that the instrument would become faulty during the Sabbath, and the player would forget the *halachic* prohibition of repairing on the Sabbath.

The spiritual leaders' attitudes regarding music could be found in several of their edicts. Rav Huna zealously prohibited all secular music in the Babylonian Jewish community and this brought about a crisis in the market place, for without music, festive celebrations stopped. Becoming aware of the decree's danger, Rav Chisda cancelled the ruling. Nevertheless, restrictions were made as to which occasions were appropriate for instrumental music and to what degree it could be used. Thus, instruments were forbidden not only on Sabbath and festivals but also on weekdays. They were, however, permitted at joyous occasions such as weddings. Even then, to prevent over-indulgence in hilarity, a dish would be thrown and broken in front of the bride and groom to remind them of the destruction of the Temple. This dish breaking tradition can be traced back to Talmudic times. When prominent sages saw an overabundance of gaiety at a wedding, they would suddenly break the most costly dishes in order to shock the guests and thus tone down the joy. This action is still replicated today before the wedding ceremony and at its conclusion. After the *t'naim* (nuptial agreement) is witnessed, the mothers of the bride and groom hold and break a plate and the bridegroom shatters a glass at the end of the wedding ceremony.

Through the centuries, the prohibitions against both instrumental and vocal music outside the synagogue were kept. With the exception of the synagogues of the Reform Movement and their use of the organ, the prohibition was never violated in the framework of the synagogue ritual.

Most communities, however, completely ignored this edict when religious events and celebrations took place in homes or even in synagogues on weekdays or at the close of the Sabbath.

It is interesting to note that during weddings and other festive occasions, older Jews from the Yemenite community beat on oil cans and copper trays in order to facilitate and accompany dancing. Because these were not considered musical instruments, they did not fall under a long-standing prohibition against the use of musical instruments issued by Islamic spiritual leaders. Although many Moslem communities defied this prohibition, it seems to have been strictly observed throughout Yemen. However, no Jewish community in the Diaspora kept the prohibition in tact and refrained from hiring musicians to add to their festivities on joyous occasions. At present, in keeping with the never formally rescinded prohibition, Jewish weddings held within the walls of the Old City of Jerusalem use only one instrument, a *tof* (drum) to accompany the merriment. Those wishing to use melodic instruments are wed outside the walled city.

Although the Destruction is the chief reason cited for refraining from music or any of its related arts, it was also the inherent nature and influential power of music that prompted the prohibition. The positions became polarized as evidenced by the following :

> When the Temple was destroyed it was decreed not to play any instrument of music or sing any songs, and all who sing songs are forbidden to be joyful and it is forbidden to let them be heard because of the destruction, as written: The elders have ceased from the gate, the young men from their music. Song is forbidden to cross the lips unless it is in the praise of the Almighty. And above all, musical instruments are forbidden at feasts; they are prohibited even if there is no feast.

The statement stresses the motivating force behind the prohibition to mourn for the destruction of the Temple. The mourning must be real and perpetual, apparent even in the circumstances calling for joy such as that evoked by a wedding reception. At all times one must share in Israel's sorrow and never forget that the *Sh'chino* (the Divine Presence) has been exiled from the Land of Israel. Music in all forms is identified with joy—the very antithesis of grief. Joy and music are for the future in the time of total redemption as in the passage "Then was our mouth filled with laughter and our tongue with singing" (Ps. 226:2). This stern approach conflicts with the basic outlook of Hasidism which particularly stresses joy in worship and ecstasy induced by song and dance. "By means of song you will achieve joy and ecstasy. One who is fearful will allay his fears with songs of joy. And faith too has its own special songs. "This coincides with the words of the *Zohar* (The Book of Splendor), "for, indeed, we see that the Divinity is not present in a place of sadness but in a place of joy. Where there is no joy, the Divinity does not rest."

SYNAGOGUE SONG OF THE ASHKENAZIM

Ashkenazim refers to those Jews who lived in Western, Central and Eastern Europe and their descendants who moved to all corners of the earth. Originally, only German Jews were considered *Ashkenazim*. According to tradition, Charlemagne settled the Italian Kalonymous family in Mayence in the eighth century. He also imported the Baghdad, sage, Rabbi Machir, and settled him in Narbonne, Southern France. From that time on, Jewish learning and tradition were transplanted into France and Germany. During the 10th and 11th centuries, the immigration of oriental rabbis into France was considerable, and they brought with them their oriental traditions. These became the basis for the religious practices of Jews in both France and Germany.

Before 1000 CE almost no differences existed between the Old French and the Old German rituals because both were founded on the *Amram* ritual. Rashi, in the 11th century, states that "all our religious customs are according to the Babylonian tradition." The same may be assumed for the synagogue song. The close relationship between Jews and Gentiles in early centuries, especially during the reign of Charlemagne and his son, Louis the Pious, brought about a cultural interchange in which the Jews were more frequently the influencers than the influenced.

In 825, Bishop Agobard, in a series of letters, began a campaign against the Jewish influence which, in his opinion, endangered the Christian faith. He complained that Christians attended Jewish services and preferred the blessings and prayers of the Jewish rabbis. It was well known that Christians attended Jewish meals on the Sabbath and that Christian women rested on the Sabbath and worked on Sundays. Many Christians openly declared that they would like to have a lawgiver such as Moses and had the "audacity to announce that the Jewish religion is the only true one."

In view of these facts, Agobard demanded that no man or woman attend Jewish services, observe Sabbath, participate in Jewish festival meals and that in general, Christians should stay away from Jews. Judging from the zealous tones in which these letters were written, it must be assumed that the Jewish influence was deeply felt. Restrictions against relations between Christians and Jews were issued, and old ones from the fourth and seventh centuries were renewed. At the same time, the civil and human rights of the Jews were reduced until the Jews were declared strangers and dangerous individuals.

It is an acknowledged fact that the standards of German song and music were extremely low. In the early centuries of their sojourn there, Jews exerted an influence upon their neighbors, for their cultural standards were infinitely higher than those of the latter. In the 12th century, opposition arose to the exchange of synagogue and church melodies. A Jew was forbidden to teach a cleric or Gentile layman any type of synagogue tune. Likewise it was strictly forbidden for a Gentile nurse to sing a Christian lullaby to a Jewish child. The prohibitions, however, could not stop the reciprocal exchanges, and Jews continued to study liturgical books and to sing from them. Rabbi Simeon the Great (11th century) adopted a hymn for himself, the tune of Magdala, which he claimed had been taught to him in a dream. Centuries later a revered master, The Seer of Lublin, also taught his Hasidim a similar tune which he claimed had been taught to him by the angels while he "sojourned in heaven."

Documentation attests, that, as late as the fifteenth century, Christians including dukes and their entire courts, continued to attend services in the synagogue. This reciprocal relationship lasted until the seventeenth century when Joseph Hahn, a rabbi and *chazan* who served the Jewish community of Frankfort, complained that Jews adopted Christian tunes for their Sabbath *Z'mirot* and justified their act with the excuse that the Christians had borrowed these same tunes from the Holy Temple.

Almost all the rabbis in the period between the 10th and 14th centuries, composed poems and hymns for the synagogue. They would create or adapt melodies for their poetry, and many of them became popular throughout the German congregations. Others fell into oblivion. In very rare cases, German tunes without any Jewish flavor became popular in the synagogue, at least in the early period of German Jewry.

Ashkenazic rabbis conceived the idea of expressing the significance of every holy day by distinctive tunes. The intent was to give musical expression to the underlying idea of the day by a leading motif, mode or tune assigned to it. Thus the leading motifs for *Rosh Hashana* expresses reverence and awe; those for *Yom Kippur* pleading and contrition; those for the Three Festivals joy, hope, liberty, exultation and thanksgiving; those for *Tisha B'av* mourning and so on. Upon entering the synagogue, Jews were inspired by the dominating melody or mode which served to remind them of the purpose of the day. The fact that only these out of many tunes became popular and "traditional," points to their combination of German and Jewish musical strands as the reason for their preservation.

The idea of special modes and tunes for prayers is not original or unique with *Ashkenazim*. This custom is also found in the oriental synagogue where Yemenite Jews have a special mode for the High Holidays. The Sephardim use a special *t'fila* mode for the High Holidays and special tunes for the various festivals. Neither of these communities, however, succeeded in creating a new genre of "special tunes," as did the *Ashkenazim*.

During the latter part of the medieval era, the musical output of the Jews reached a point of stagnation. This was due primarily to the desperate social position into which the Jews were forced beginning with the 13th century. The German community, at first culturally inferior, became superior, and the Jews, impoverished by cruel persecutions, were influenced by the songs of their oppressors. Beginning with the 16th century, the synagogue became Germanized. All melodies and musical compositions during this period had typical German characteristics but little "Jewish" flavor.

The music may give us a clue to the attitude of the spiritual leaders towards the tunes newly introduced into the synagogue. In the late 16th century, complaints were leveled against the *chazanim* for abandoning the old "sanctified" tunes. *Chazanim* were castigated for neglecting their traditional functions and the study of Jewish lore. They were accused of displaying their singing and art by using tunes which had no relation to the prayer texts. In addition, *chazanim* chose to officiate only during the *Musaph* service (a practice which lasted throughout the period of the Golden Age of Cantors) because this service offered them a greater opportunity to display their art. They considered the *Shacharit* and *Mincha* services of the Sabbath day beneath their dignity.

This change took place at the same time that the Protestant movement abolished Gregorian Chant and replaced it with the German folk song i.e. the hymn. The new tunes introduced into the synagogue aroused much opposition. Many religious leaders felt that adaptations of German folk tunes expressed sentiments which were not their own. The Jews in medieval Germany certainly had sentiments quite different from those of their persecutors. Even the hopes that the Jews had placed in the liberal Protestants had turned to bitter disappointment.

Throughout its history, the Catholic Church made an effort to preserve the traditional song of the church, and to keep away the "vulgar secular tunes." Unfortunately, no major efforts were issued to this end in the synagogue. The Jew was guided primarily by his instinct, and, as long as Jewish culture was strong, wherever he developed his spiritual culture and lived accordingly, his religious song was Jewish.

During the period of flourishing Jewish culture in Germany, the rabbi paid much attention to the ritual of the synagogue. The last prominent rabbi to render great service to the synagogue song was Jacob Levi Molin, known as the *Maharil* (1356-1427). Considered to be the greatest rabbinical authority of his time, he felt that the communities should hold fast to their traditional customs and melodies. When the spiritual life of German Jews began to decay in the 14th century, the *Maharil*, by his exalted personality, saved the synagogue ritual when he sanctioned the old tunes.

In spite of the great influence of the *Maharil*, the spirit of the Ashkenazic service was greatly affected by the persecutions of the 15th and 16th centuries, when communities were attacked or partially expelled. The German Jew, hated and enslaved during the course of the week, wanted to forget himself and be refreshed on the Sabbath and Festivals with popular songs. Therefore, despite the protestations of the rabbinic leaders, the congregation urged the *chazan* to satisfy its desires through popular songs of the day. In fact, they demanded that the *chazan* sing the religious texts of the service to these outside secular tunes.

The recurring difficulties and expulsions produced an unsettled Jewish community life, and many congregations eliminated the position of permanent *chazan*. The *chazan* was forced to wander from city to city giving concerts and performing services. He assumed a minstrel-like character, resembling that of the wandering Italian musicians of the time who overran central Europe. As a result of the political and cultural circumstances, and partly influenced by the "wandering music makers," the *chazan* abandoned all functions connected with his office, and confined himself to his music, constructing dazzling tunes in order to catch the attention of the masses. To put an end to this activity, Rabbi Moses Minz, at the request of the old community of Bamberg, wrote detailed regulations for the *chazan* which included the *chazan's* behavior in the synagogue, his manner of conduct with members of the synagogue, and concern with the dignity of the sacred office.

Those communities fortunate enough to escape the brutalities of the Christian clergy and the mob, continued the dignity and tradition of the synagogue. Consequently, their *minhag* became the standard for the ravaged communities which attempted to re-establish their religious practices. By the end of the 16th and the beginning of the 17th century, the synagogue song of the Ashkenazim was well established, and, with the exception of typical German tunes, the Ashkenazic song spread all over Eastern and Central Europe.

FROM THE PROFANE TO THE HOLY

The Jewish people are a phenomenon among the nations of the world. For more than 2000 years Jews lived in those host countries that would accept and offer them citizenship or immigrant status. Arab countries, the European continent and later the Americas, served as such hosts. In some countries Jews were partially integrated and in several, they had, for a time, full rights as citizens. That a national Jewish spirit continued unabated until the return to Israel, is one of the remarkable chapters in the history of nations.

Along the way, Jews discovered an essential tool for cultural survival—the adoption of elements from their surroundings. Adopting foreign elements, however, necessitated the simultaneous act of adaptation. In keeping with the Biblical injunction *b'chukotéhem lo téléchu* one must not do exactly as non-Jews do, those items that were adopted, were reworked or "Judaized." In dress, for example, certain popular and fashionable items of clothing were transformed into religious garments. Beginning in the late 18th century, Hasidic leaders adopted the Polish and Russian winter fur hat. By reconstructing the hat with thirteen fur tails (corresponding to the thirteen attributes of God), the head covering became a *shtreimel*. The *shtreimel*, unlike its fur hat predecessor, was not worn casually on weekdays, but only on the Sabbath, holidays and specific celebratory events such as weddings and circumcisions. The Prince Albert style frock coat, an elegant garment popular in European society, was modified and emerged among Hasidim as a *capote*. The *capote* became standard garb for many Hasidic and other Orthodox Jews and is worn to this day.

For the Jewish community during the Golden Age in Spain, Hebrew remained the language of prayer and the Bible. The spoken language of the Jews, however, was Spanish with the addition of phrases borrowed from Hebrew. Known as Ladino or "Judezmo," this became the common language of Spanish Jewry and their descendants. After the Expulsion from Spain in

1492, Ladino remained a spoken language for the Jews who settled in the Mediterranean and Balkan countries. Many Sephardic synagogues world-wide still include liturgical prayers recited in Ladino in their Sabbath and Festival services. Yiddish, another borrowed language, was based on German and contained Hebrew, Aramaic, Polish, and Russian as well as words and phrases of other languages. Yiddish was the spoken language of European Jewry and remains a viable language especially among Orthodox and Hasidic Jews.

In addition to borrowing language, dress, and ethnic foods, Jews did not hesitate to adopt foreign melodies which they added to their own long-standing musical tradition. Should Jews find the notion of adopting philosophically problematical, they should be aware that borrowing, especially in music, was not a one-way affair. From earliest times, cross-cultural borrowing of music was in place. Pope Gregory the Great (6th century AD) used the music of the synagogue as one of his primary sources when collecting and codifying music, now known as *Gregorian Chant*, for the Church. A number of centuries later, the close relationship between Jews and Gentiles, especially during the reign of Charlemagne and his son, Louis the Pious, brought about a cultural interchange in which the Jews were more frequently the influencers than the influenced.

Almost every folk music contains foreign elements. A study of French folk songs will show strains of Italian music, while Romanian motifs can be detected in Hungarian music. Slavic influence is evident in German folk songs, and French strains appear in the music of northern Spain. The contacts between the various lands, the relationships between countries, the wars that occurred, all had a share in bringing about this musical cross-pollination and hybridization. Hasidic leaders not only allowed the borrowing of melodies from the host culture, but they advocated and urged their adherents to take secular melodies and make them "holy" by adapting them to liturgical texts for the synagogue service. They considered this act to be an exemplary *mitzvah*, that of turning the profane into the holy. The leaders felt that this was similar to turning a house of pagan worship into a synagogue. Often a Rebbe would proclaim a foreign tune worthy of being chosen for inclusion in a sacred service. He would issue instructions to redeem the *nitsotz shel k'dusha* (the spark of holiness) of the foreign folk melody and incorporate it into the repertoire of his group. It is related among the *Karlin* Hasidim that at the funeral of Czar Nikolai, their Rebbe, Rabbi Israel, his son and several disciples were all standing together. During the proceedings, a song was sung that the rabbi told his disciples would be worthwhile to adopt for the psalm, *Mizmor Shir Chanukat Habayit* (Consecration of the House). Subsequently, it was customary among the *Karlin* Hasidim to sing this song during the Hanukah festival or when celebrating a house warming.

With regard to motifs and styles, it must also be remembered that Jews created their music in foreign cultures and that no creation can truly be called original if it does not grow in its national homeland. Only through the spiritual homeland that Jews created were they able to infuse their musical soul into some of the foreign currents. Later, with far less success, Hasidim, notably those of *Kotzk* and *Ger*, made use of the melodies of Schubert, Chopin and Verdi. That these melodies have been completely forgotten by the Hasidim is the best indication that they did not lend themselves to a reworking in the Hasidic mold.

Not unlike the Hasidic Rebbes, but with different motivation, the Reform Rabbinate in Germany of the 19th century urged its cantors to glean melodies from the German folk repertoire and use these tunes in the synagogue by adapting them to liturgical texts. The rabbis hoped that this borrowing would bring about a *brüdershaft* (brotherhood), a common bond between the Jews and their German neighbors, through shared melodies. Thus, a number of church style hymns, such as the famous melody for *Ma'oz Tsur* (Rock of Ages), which became one of the most popular of all Jewish songs, entered the repertoire.

WANDERING MINSTRELS

Reports from the Middle Ages tell about Jewish minstrels and jugglers who, regardless of the rabbinic prohibitions against secular music, roamed the countryside performing before both Jews and Gentiles. In general, the wandering artist had a very low status in medieval society. Among Christians, he was almost an outcast, and often regarded with the same suspicion, as were the Jews. Nevertheless, minstrelsy was an old vocation which had spread over the continent in the path of the Roman legions. Jews found and joined the universally open class of minstrels. This way of life continued for many Jews throughout the Middle Ages and beyond. Jewish communities themselves could not afford the luxury of offering a livelihood to this kind of artist. In addition to reciting long epic poems, the minstrels provided entertainment by dancing, rope walking, knife throwing, as well as singing and playing. Since the wandering artist was considered an outsider in any case, his Jewish extraction was of very little consequence. It was, therefore, not uncommon to find a Jew as the court musician of a caliph, emir, Christian king, bishop or knight.

The kings of Spain held Jewish musicians in high esteem. They are repeatedly mentioned in the court accounts of 14th-16th centuries. These musicians were welcome because they added flavor to the sometimes rather dull court atmosphere. They received considerable remuneration and were granted very pompous titles. "El Ropero" the son of a Jewish tailor was maliciously called "cohen" and "judio" by his rivals but was nevertheless allowed to address Queen Isabella with a protest song against the persecution of the Marranos in 1473. One of his Jewish contemporaries, Juan of Valladolid, was court musician at the Spanish court of Naples.

The activities of Jewish singers immediately before the expulsion from Spain testifies that they were outsiders in every respect, regarded neither as Jews nor Christians. They also appeared in the company of troubadours and trouvers, and like Suesskind of Trimberg (c. 1220), these Jewish singers mastered the international repertoire no less than their Gentile colleagues. In addition, they performed subject matter from the Bible and *Midrash*.

The Jewish wandering minstrels served as intermediaries between the ghettos and their environment. They were also the bearers of an instrumental tradition, especially in the field of dance music. They brought to the Jewish quarter the music of the Gentile weddings and other happy occasions, and it was not unusual for some of these dance melodies to find their way into synagogue song. It must be understood that it was the broad masses of people who regulated musical taste by either giving or denying approval of certain melodies to the *chazan*. Conditions in the Jewish exile often did not allow for refined art, and time and again Jews were thrown back to the level of poor people, and to the music enjoyed by such.

Susskind von Trimberg (13th cent. Manasser Codex.)

DANCING

From time immemorial dancing was used by nations in an attempt to ward off evil spirits, threatening diseases, or droughts. Often dance served as a prelude to battle. Historically, dance was always an important and often spiritual activity within Judaism. At the Exodus, after crossing the Red Sea, Miriam, the sister of Aaron, took a timbrel in her hand and was followed by all the women with timbrels and with dancing. After the victory of Jephtah over the Ammonites, his daughter came towards him with drums and dancing. When David defeated the Philistines, the women came out from all the cities of Israel to sing and dance before King Saul. Both the Prophets and the Talmud relate how girls used to dance on the Festivals, on Tu B'av, and on Yom Kippur. At the Water Libation ceremony, held during the festival of *Sukot*, men danced before the people with torches in their hands. Throughout the Middle Ages, although beset by major problems caused by the host countries, Jews danced.

Soon after the Black Death (1348-49), an "Epidemic of Dancing" spread throughout Germany. Especially in the Rhineland, hundreds of men and women danced to utter exhaustion. Lasting until the beginning of the fifteenth century, this epidemic carried over into the Jewish ghettos, where a *Tanzhaus* (a hall for dancing) was found. Weddings took place in the *Tanzhaus*, and, during the holidays, Christian instrumentalists were permitted to play while Jews danced. Although the rabbis in Germany were not in favor of these practices, the dancing halls soon spread throughout France and Germany, until one could be found in most Jewish communities.

In Safed, Palestine, the center of Kabbalah until the year sixteen hundred, groups performed song and dance at the end of Sabbath in Jewish homes throughout the community. In addition, the older generation participated in mixed couples dancing in the style of their adoptive country. Rabbi Yehudah Hahasid attempted to put an end to this activity by decreeing that mixed dancing among the youth must cease but that religious Jewish dance by separated sexes could continue.

The Dance of Miriam. From a 14th cent. Spanish Haggadah

Rikud (dance), which can bring about ecstasy, is one of the fundamentals of Hasidism. Rabbi Nachman of Bratslav taught his followers that every part of the body had a rhythm of its own "as the melody brings out the beauty in poetry, the dance brings it to a climax." Rabbi Nachman, who often danced, said that the root of blessing is found in dance. His dancing was so ecstatic that Bratslaver Hasidim proclaimed, "He, who did not see his dancing, saw no other good during his lifetime."

It is related among Hasidim, that a Rabbi Shabtai, who lived during the time of the Baal Shem Tov, was extremely poor, and all of his weekly efforts were dedicated to obtaining minimum food necessary for the celebration of the Sabbath. Though the results of his efforts usually proved meager, Rabbi

Shabtai nevertheless was joyous and sang and danced with ecstasy in honor of the Sabbath. From afar, the Baal Shem Tov was able to see Rabbi Shabtai dancing and said, "Because of his ecstatic dancing, Rabbi Shabtai will father a son who will light up the eyes of all of Israel." Shabtai's son grew up to be Rabbi Israel, the Magid of Koznitz.

Unfortunately, some of the most violent criticism leveled against Hasidim by their opponents, the *misnagdim*, was the fact that they were always singing, dancing, clapping their hands, and emitting wild cries during prayers, "which is entirely against Jewish tradition." Dancing was not only encouraged by the Hasidic movement but, along with song, was incorporated into religious observance and even into the liturgy. This was in keeping with the Psalmist who said, *ivdu et Hashem b'simcha* (serve God with joy). The need for joy led the Baal Shem Tov to teach his pupils not to inhibit themselves during prayers. He instructed them to move their bodies about freely, shaking and rocking from side to side, so that they could also fulfill *kol atsmosai tomarna* (all parts of my body shall proclaim), as stated in the prayer, *Nishmat*, found in the Sabbath and Festival morning liturgy.

Thus, Hasidim rarely stood still during prayers, and the Rebbes and their followers injected bodily movements and actual dance steps wherever possible. These dance movements combined spontaneity with profound inner exaltation and were mainly improvised by the dancers, who expressed their individual ecstatic experiences either alone or in groups, without any intention to show off or to entertain.

There were special dances for the Sabbath, and, among the followe rs of the Beshtian School, it was customary for the entire village to go out, singing and dancing, to welcome the Sabbath Queen. The Sabbath Eve hymn, *L'cho Dodi* (Come My Beloved), composed by Solomon Ben Moses Halevi Alkabetz (1505-1580), was the vehicle for this mystical-devotional processional.

The singing of *L'cho Dodi* continued the tradition established by the Kabbalists of Safed who, long before the birth of Hasidism, went out every Friday afternoon in a procession over the hills of Galilee to welcome the

Sabbath Queen with songs and dances. The custom of dancing during the *L'cho Dodi* has been retained in a number of Hasidic synagogues to this day. This is especially true of the Bratslav Hasidim, where dancing takes place not only in the synagogue, but often, during favorable weather conditions, on the street.

Dance was also at the center of the *Hakofos* (Procession of the Scrolls) on *Simchat Torah* when the Rebbe would dance wrapped in his *talis* (prayer shawl), carrying the Torah close to his heart. The Rebbe would pour out his ecstatic feelings in a rapturous dance while his followers formed a circle around him singing appropriate *nigunim* and clapping their hands rhythmically. At first, Hasidic dances were performed only in the prayer-houses, but, later, such dances took place outside the synagogues for occasions such as weddings, circumcisions, or the commemoration of a notable event in the life of a beloved *Tsadik*. Hasidim who emigrated to Palestine danced annually at the grave of Rabbi Shimon Bar Yochai, a direct descendant of Moses and the author of the *Zohar*.

At times Hasidim indulged in rather curious customs. The followers of Rabbi Aaron of Karlin (d. 1792) used to roll on the ground in rhythm each morning before the *Shacharis* service. They were known as *kulyikes* (rollers) and were highly praised by the congregation for their devoted and saintly practice. In a moment of ecstatic fervor, some Hasidim turned upside down and walked with their hands. When the fervor left them, they returned to normal walking. Dancing figured prominently in an elaborate ceremony conducted in the synagogue of the Magid of Kozhnitz when he came to pray. He entered the synagogue carrying a Torah scroll and was accompanied by two attendants bearing lighted candles. The first candle was placed near the platform and the second on the pulpit. The Rebbe then danced opposite the Holy Ark, three dance steps forward and three backward. Then he placed the little scroll into the Holy Ark and once more danced three steps forward and three backward. Only then did the Rebbe begin to pray. As he prayed, he danced with such fire and inspiration, that, when he was almost done, he fell away in a faint. Then the Rebbe, who was very frail, was wrapped in lambskin, and carried back to his private chamber, worn out and exhausted from his ecstatic dancing.

In most Hasidic communities, the *mitsve tants* is the final public event of a wedding. In Hasidic sources, the *mitsve tants* has a certain mystical significance and is described as a symbolic unification of a celestial bride and groom and, as a result, that of the earthly couple. The *mitsve tants* is danced to a number of traditional melodies and is directed by one individual, who invites some of the guests to dance with the bride. The bride and groom are seated and, as each guest is called, the bride stands. When the Rebbe is present, he is invited to dance first. The grandfathers dance after the Rebbe, and they are followed by the fathers and, finally, the groom. Each guest invited to dance holds one end of a kerchief or *gartle* (sash) while the bride holds the other end. As the *nigun* is sung, only the guest dances, sometimes with closed eyes, using a simple circle dance step pattern. The bride hardly moves at all, but may take a few steps when her father or bridegroom dances with her. After several steps the guest drops the sash or kerchief and is joined by the other men present, in a circle-dance, while the bride returns to her chair beside the groom. The groom is last to dance with the bride. They hold hands, take several steps, and then the groom is drawn back into the men's circle. The Rebbe does not dance the *mitsve tants* in the regular fashion. He stands in front of the bride and moves forward and backward in quick short steps. In Hasidic sources, this type of dancing is called *rotso voshov* (running back and forth). This term is full of mystical connotations referring to man's attempt to come closer to God. After the dance the guests wish good luck and bid "good night" to one another and the wedding is over.

Since the Baal Shem Tov founded his movement, Hasidic dancing has been performed predominantly by males. Although women would at times engage in small circle dances in a confined area, the men made dancing a prime religious activity. During the last quarter of the 20th century, *simcha* dancing by women only, has become popular and can be seen at most traditional Jewish weddings held in Orthodox and Hasidic communities. For these affairs, the dance floor is often divided by a *mechitza* (partition) so that the male and female dancing takes place in separate areas.

It is likely that *simcha* dancing developed as a reaction to women's need to dance at festive occasions. *Simcha* dancing, however, progressed and became a studied and programmed dance formula. Dance classes given by "professionals" were regularly held, and instructional videotapes, audiocassettes and compact discs made available to the market place. Borrowed primarily from American culture, such dances as the "Salty Dog Rag" have been adopted. Conforming to the process of adoption and adaptation, however, modification in the steps were made in order to "Judaize" these borrowed dances. While the men usually dance in large or concentric circles, the women dance singly in straight lines, and no part of their bodies comes in contact with their neighbors on the dance floor.

Joy Among Hasidim by Tully Filmus

SALAMONE ROSSI

Influenced by the Renaissance, Italian Jews began to enter musical life and contribute to European composition. Excluded from social circles and without human rights, some Jewish musicians nevertheless were privileged at the court of the art-loving Dukes of Mantua during the second half of the 16th and the first quarter of the 17th century. Salamone Rossi (1565?-1628) was the most gifted and famous Jewish musician at the court of Mantua. Better known to his Jewish brethren as *Schelomo Me-ha-adumim* (Solomon the Redhead), Rossi claimed to be a descendant of a prominent family that could be traced back to the captives of Jerusalem brought to Rome by Titus. For more than forty years, he was a composer, singer and violinist at the ducal court. His sister, Madama Europa, a singer and actress, was also famous and his nephew, Anselmi Rossi, was employed as a court musician.

In addition to playing the viol at the court of Mantua from 1587 to 1622, Rossi was a prolific composer who was held in high regard by his contemporaries. He was invited by princes to present concerts at their courts and enjoyed such favor that in 1606 he was permitted to dispense with the yellow badge that all Jews were ordered to wear at the time.

However important and pioneering his activity in the field of Renaissance music may have been, primary Jewish interest in Rossi lies in the fact that he also devoted his considerable talents to the synagogue. In a bold and unprecedented move in the history of Jewish music, he undertook to "reform" synagogue music. His reform did not mean purifying the traditional music of the synagogue. Rather, he began composing and introducing entirely new music in the style of his time.

Rabbi Leon Modena, one of the most universally gifted figures of the Renaissance, was a schooled singer and musician. He was one of Rossi's staunchest supporters and with four rabbinical colleagues wrote a responsum, or expert opinion, in which he demonstrated that according to rabbinic law, there should be no objection to the use of music, new or old. In 1605 Modena himself organized choirs of six and eight voices in the Italian synagogue of Ferrara, conducted according to "musical science" i.e. harmony. Although strong opposition arose to this innovation, Modena submitted the case to the rabbinical assembly in Venice which decided that it was permissible.

Rossi did not intend to adapt synagogue music to the trend of his time. His aim was to create an entirely new style for liturgical music. He composed 33 Psalms titled *Hashirim Asher Lishlomo* (a play on *Shir Hashirim*, the *Song of Songs*), and they were printed in Venice (1622). Rossi's dedication states that it was his aim "to glorify and beautify the songs of King David according to the rules of music." Rabbi Modena, who proofread the manuscript, wrote a preface in Hebrew. This apology was aimed at winning over the rabbis, most of whom had completely opposed the innovation. The music was printed in parts, not as a complete score, with the Hebrew texts running the opposite way of his music. Rossi's compositions were intended only for particular occasions such as special Sabbaths or festivals and were not meant to replace the traditional synagogue chants.

It is not certain how long Rossi's music lasted in the synagogue, but we do know that it was not long lived. In 1630 Mantua was swept by war and captured by Ferdinado II. Jews were expelled from the city in 1800. The glorious era ceased for Jews in northern Italy; soon Rossi's music was forgotten and the Italian synagogue went back to the old traditional songs with more zeal than ever. In the same synagogue in Ferrara, where one hundred and forty years earlier a choir had sung "new music," someone dared to change the traditional musical setting of the *Birkat Kohanim* (the Blessing of the Priests), and was excommunicated by the Ferrara rabbinate.

Although Rossi's songs vanished from the Italian Synagogue, they nevertheless exerted an influence by arousing an interest in elaborate music in Germany. Indirectly, Rossi's efforts and introduction of the Italian style influenced the 17th and 18th century synagogue in central Europe. Choral singing in parts and even instrumental music in the synagogue were accepted. His music was not issued in complete score until it was re-edited and published in 1877 by the composer Samuel Naumbourg. Due to the sincere efforts of a number of choral conductors, especially in the United States and Europe, Rossi's *Hashirim Asher Lishlomo* are once again heard in synagogues, concert halls and in choral performances.

Barchu

44

SYNAGOGUE SONG-16th, 17th & 18th centuries

At the beginning of the 16th century, the Renaissance spirit penetrated the ghetto and aroused the artistic temperament of the *chazanim*. From Italy, singers and musicians spread their new art throughout northern Europe. Under the spell of these minstrels, the *chazanim* abandoned their traditional functions and devoted themselves completely to music, traveling from community to community in order to perform their concert services. Writing about this, Rabbi Herz Treves (1470-1550) complains:

> They have ceased to be writers of the *Torah, t'filin, m'gilot*; nor do they care for the correct grammatical reading nor for the meaning of the prayer, only for their songs, without regard to the real sense of the words.
> They neglect the traditional tunes of their ancestors.

While Italy saw the fight between Leon of Modena and the majority of rabbis over the introduction of music into the synagogue (see Salamone Rossi), Prague equipped its new sanctuary (1594) with an organ. In addition, an instrumental group was specially organized to play and accompany specific songs including *L'cha Dodi* on Friday evening before sunset. Similar concerts were held in most of the nine synagogues in Prague. At the beginning of the 18th century, there were reports of instrumental music in the communities of Nikolsburg, Offenbach, and Furth.

There was a twofold reason for the instrumental concerts that took place before the services. Rabbi Isaac Luria, and the Kabbalists under his leadership, placed much stress on receiving the Sabbath with song. Accordingly, his disciples composed special melodies for the occasion. Outside the Kabbalist enclave, instrumental music concerts before the Sabbath took place in many synagogues throughout Europe at the beginning of the 17th century. In similar fashion, the German Protestant Church performed instrumental and choral selections with instrumental accompaniment before Sunday morning service. This performance was known as "religious concert" or "cantata." Throughout the 17th and 18th centuries, Jewish musicians volunteered to play in congregations on Friday evening for about an hour. In 1793, the custom was abolished in all the Prague synagogues because the musicians often continued to play after sunset thereby breaking the laws of Sabbath.

MISINAI TUNES

Ashkenaz Jewry created a new genre of special "sanctified" melodies known as *scarbove*. The derivation and the meaning of the word *scarbove* are, according to Idelsohn (see Abraham Zvi Idelsohn), a corruption of the Latin *sacra* (sacred). A dissenting view by the musicologist Alfred Sendrey held that the word is derived from the Polish *skarb* (treasure) and *scarbove* therefore means from the treasure. Generically, these melodies became known as the *Misinai* (from Mount Sinai) tunes. The birthplace of these melodies was Southwestern Germany, in the communities of Worms, Mayence, Speyer and the Rhineland. The name *Misinai*, is an indication of the veneration with which these melodies were held. Perhaps the origin of the term can be found in the volume *Sefer Hasidim* in which the assertion is made that some of these songs were given to Moses at Mount Sinai.

The melodies belonging to this category, and still adhered to in all Ashkenaz synagogues world wide, accompany liturgical texts from the High Holidays and the Festivals. They include *Bar'chu* (evening service of the High Holidays), *Hamelech*, *Avot* (High Holiday morning service), *Kol Nidre* (Yom Kippur evening), *V'hakohanim*, *Alenu* (Yom Kippur *Musaf*), the various melodies for the *Kaddish* recited before High Holiday *Musaf*, Yom Kippur *N'ilah*, and the *Tal* (Dew) and *Geshem* (Rain) prayers, recited during the Passover and *Sukot* festivals respectively.

KOL NIDRE

A long-standing fable still exists with regard to *Kol Nidre*. Many otherwise knowledgeable Jews believe that both the text and the melody of this prayer emerged from the Spanish Inquisition. They assume that the *Kol Nidre*, essentially a formula for self-absolution, was specifically designed to free those who had been forcibly converted, from their imposed obligations. In a vivid, but imaginary scene, the Marranos are seen gathering clandestinely in cellars or catacombs for the sacred service of the Day of Atonement. The Inquisitors watch everywhere and the congregants are potential martyrs, for discovery means sure death. Despite the danger facing them, the Marranos realize the holiness of the day and are determined to remain faithful to their ancestral tradition. This determination conquers the terror, which the possibility of discovery might inspire, and from their hearts the melody of *Kol Nidre* bursts forth.

To this imaginary picture has been added a number of variations. In an essay, Cantor Pinchas Minkovksy, a recognized author and musical scholar, wrote

> And when we sing the *Kol Nidre*, it is not the dry legalistic formula of absolution, which stirs us. We are exalted by the memory of those crypto-Jews, hidden in cave and catacomb, wrapped in their *tallithim*, (prayer shawls) and engaged in their prayer. We see them again, fear upon their countenances, and in their hearts a pure devotion and an overwhelming desire to annul the vows and oaths which the agents of Torquemada had forced upon them.

Subsequently Minkovsky did correct himself and, in a second essay, he approached the Spanish legend in an entirely different manner. He adopted the opposite extreme and tried to prove that the *Kol Nidre* melody cannot claim great antiquity because it displays tonal peculiarities that do not appear in music before the Renaissance.

In Volume V, of his *Thesaurus of Oriental Melodies*, A.Z. Idelsohn notes that the *Sephardim*, the true heirs of the *Marranos*, sing *Kol Nidre* with a melody which differs entirely from that sung by *Ashkenazim*. Quite possibly, in reference to the essay in *Hashiloach*, he

47

indulges in some sarcasm at the expense of "one of the cantors of Eastern Europe."

The melody of the *Kol Nidre*, as it is sung by the Sephardim, has its roots in the melody with which the Sephardim intone the *S'lichot*; it has not the slightest relationship to the Ashkenazic *Kol Nidre* melody. And as for the fairy tale that this melody originated with the Marranos and was uttered by them in fear and in holiness as they gathered for the sacred service in their places of hiding, it is pure fantasy which inspired one of the cantors of Eastern Europe to promote this highly imaginative hypothesis. "

The text and the chant of *Kol Nidre* was formally introduced by Rabbi Yehudai Gaon (740 CE), but it seems that it had a different function at that time and most certainly a different melody. It was not repeated three times nor did it have the present day preamble *B'y'shiva shel ma'ala* (In the Academy on High). The practice of repeating the *Kol Nidre* was considered in a host of Ashkenazic rabbinic responsa. The most important by Maharil, states that the *chazan* is "to extend the chant of the *Kol Nidre* until nightfall. He must chant the *Kol Nidre* three times, first in an undertone, then louder during the first repetition and even louder for the third, for then we shall hearken with awe and trembling." Nowhere does the Maharil refer to any specific tune for the text, but speaks only of "long drawn out melodies."

The first authoritative reference to the melody comes from Rabbi Mordecai Jaffa of Prague, who was not satisfied with the version used by the *chazanim*. It seems that they corrupted and mixed the various versions of the text indiscriminately. The first version of the melody appeared in a collection of liturgical synagogue chants published in 1785 by Ahron Beer, a cantor in Berlin. Although his transcription contains most of the familiar elements, the melody continued to change. One hundred years later Louis Lewandowski transcribed the melody and it appeared in print. Many variants and arrangements appear and continue to appear. Various composers made arrangements of the *Kol Nidre* for cantor, choir and organ.

KOL NIDRE IN CONCERT

In 1826, Ludwig von Beethoven was commissioned by the Jewish community in Vienna to compose a cantata for the dedication of their new Temple. Although the composer considered this idea for a while, he later declined. The task was accomplished by his pupil, the composer Seyfried. It may very well be that, while Beethoven was considering this commission, he began to look into Jewish thematic material, and *Kol Nidre* was brought to his attention. We find the theme of *Kol Nidre* woven throughout Beethoven's *C#minor String Quartet*, opus 131, composed during that period.

Max Bruch, a nineteenth century composer, wrote a *Kol Nidre* for cello and orchestra which has become a well known show piece for virtuoso cellists. Although the composition opens with recognizable elements of the chant, it then digresses into lyric romantic passages which have almost no relationship to the original.

Far less frequently performed but much closer to the melody and spirit of the chant, is the *Kol Nidre* by the great twentieth century composer, Arnold Schoenberg. Written in 1938 for chorus, orchestra and "speaker," it had its premiere performance in 1958, seven years after the death of the composer. Schoenberg's *Kol Nidre* has an interesting history. Although born a Jew, the composer had converted to Christianity in his youth. Subsequently he shunned all religious affiliation. The Nazis drove him, along with many other great artists, to find refuge in the United States. He settled in Los Angeles where he met the noted Rabbi Jacob Sonderling. The rabbi was able to stir Schoenberg's Jewish feelings to such a degree that the composer resolved to return formally to Judaism. His "act of contrition"— symbolic of his reconversion—was this *Kol Nidre*.

Kol Nidre

Traditional
Adapted by R.J. Neumann

50

Kol nid-ré ve-e-sa-ré va-cha-ra-mé v'ko-na-mé v'chi-nu-yé v'-ki-nu-sé ush'-vu-ot. Din-dar-na ud'-ish-ta-ba-na u-d'-a-cha-rim-na v'di-a-sar-na al naf-sha-ta-na. Mi-yom ki-pu-rim ze ad yom ki-pu-rim ha-ba a-lé-nu l'-to-va. Kul-hon i-cha-rat-na v'hon kul-hon y'-hon sha-ran. Sh'vi-kin sh'vi-tin b'-té-lin u-m'vu-ta-lin la-sh'-ri-rin v'-la ka-ya-min. Nid-ra-na la nid-ré ve-e-sa-ra-na la e-sa-ré ush-vu-a-ta-na la sh'-vu-ot

כָּל נִדְרֵי · וֶאֱסָרֵי · וַחֲרָמֵי · וְקוֹנָמֵי · וְכִנּוּיֵי · וְקִנּוּסֵי · וּשְׁבוּעוֹת · דִּנְדַרְנָא · וּדְאִשְׁתַּבַּעְנָא · וּדְאַחֲרִימְנָא · וְדְאָסַרְנָא עַל נַפְשָׁתָנָא · מִיּוֹם כִּפּוּרִים זֶה עַד יוֹם כִּפּוּרִים הַבָּא עָלֵינוּ לְטוֹבָה · כֻּלְּהוֹן אִחֲרַטְנָא בְהוֹן · כֻּלְהוֹן יְהוֹן שָׁרָן · שְׁבִיקִין · שְׁבִיתִין · בְּטֵלִין וּמְבֻטָּלִין · לָא שְׁרִירִין וְלָא קַיָּמִין · נִדְרָנָא לָא נִדְרֵי · וֶאֱסָרָנָא לָא אֱסָרֵי · וּשְׁבוּעָתָנָא לָא שְׁבוּעוֹת:

Sheet music folio early 20ᵗʰ century

EAST EUROPEAN *CHAZANUTH*

One of the essential considerations in East European *chazanuth* was the cantor's voice. Like other Orientals, the Jew has always shown preference for a "sweet voice" which meant to him a lyric tenor with nasal quality rather than a baritone or bass. The tenor voice usually had the qualities required to move the heart of the Jew by means of its natural sweetness. This same lyric quality was to be found in the violin, and that became the favorite "Jewish" instrument. With very few exceptions, the great *chazanim* were tenors, and those who were not, "tenorized" their voices. (This situation was prevalent during the first half of the 20th century, especially in the Orthodox synagogue, where it was almost impossible for a baritone or bass to receive a permanent appointment as *chazan*.)

Until the 18th century, information with regard to synagogue song is scanty. It is known, however, that the cantor was required to satisfy the popular desire for music. The Jew demanded that the *chazan*, through music, make him forget his difficult daily life and elevate him on wings of song into a beautiful world. At the end of the 17th century, Rabbi Selig Margolis of Kalisch described the quality of eastern European *chazanuth* which inspired the people more than the preaching of their rabbis. He reported that people who could normally not be brought to tears or prayer by the death of a parent, were moved to tears and repentance through the touching song of a *chazan*, Boruch of Kalish. Such was the power of their singing, that a record of the Chmelnitzki pogroms in 1648 described a *chazan*, Hirsch of Ziviotov, who, through his emotional chanting of the *El Mole Rachamim* (prayer for the departed), moved the Tartars to save 3000 Jews from the hands of the rampaging Cossacks. After this pogrom, which caused the dispersion of many Jews, the *chazanim* emigrated to Central and Western Europe where they transplanted their eastern *chazanuth* and fused it with the traditional German Ashkenazic song.

Despite the antagonism towards the *ars nova* introduced by the *chazanim* in the 16th and 17th centuries and the opposition to the choir which it created, the choir became an established organization in almost every congregation and community. At the beginning of the 18th century, we find the community or *k'hal* singers consisting of a bass and a soprano or falsetto. In 1700, choirs were introduced in Amsterdam, Hamburg and Frankfurt. In Prague, every synagogue had its choral society of volunteers. In Podolia and Galicia, the institution of the choir was established at the time of the Baal Shem Tov.

Chazan, bass and singer in a Jewish service. From a Machzor (14[b] century)

For the origins, uses and abuses of the new style of song introduced by the *chazanim*, we have two sources of information— the rabbis and the *chazanim* themselves.

> The custom of the *chazan*im in our generation is to invent tunes and to transfer tunes from the secular to the sacred. They know not how to read the Torah because the congregations prefer to have *chazan*im show off with sweet voices and fine singing. Every Sabbath the number of new tunes increases–tunes, which we knew not before.

Two *chazanim*, Yehuda Leib ben Moses and Solomon Lifshitz, both testified that the cantors incorporated tunes from the theatre or dance halls into the service. Other *chazanim* were accused of taking tunes from the Catholic Church. It is interesting to note that Rabbi Joel Sirkes. a great rabbinical authority, responded that there was no objection whatsoever, so long as the tunes had not been used for the Christian service. By this judgment, he pronounced secular tunes permissible.

The invasion of the *ars nova* into the synagogue and the custom of adopting or imitating secular music was paralleled by the same procedure in the church. Tunes, vulgar in spirit, arias, minuets, melodies belonging in the theater were introduced into the church, lasting throughout the 18th century. The borrowing of secular tunes by the church was an old custom. In earlier times, however, the secular folk song was closer to Gregorian Chant in spirit. During a later period, especially in the 17th and 18th century, the folk song and secular music influenced the church song to the extent that it departed from the traditional chorale style and adopted the secular style. Thus, we see that the church lived through the same struggle as did the synagogue.

East European cantors

THE GOLDEN AGE OF CANTORS

Although little documentation of the period commonly refered to as the "Golden Age of Cantors" is available, it is possible to piece together information from articles printed in cantorial souvenir journals and personal interviews. In the early 1900's, the few American cantors with permanent synagogue positions were to be found primarily in New York City. Although renumeration at the time was quite low, these cantors were able to exist on meager compensation because many of the amenities now taken for granted were not available. Electricity, steam heat, refrigeration (and their costs) were not yet in widespread use, even in wealthier homes, and, if a cantor was frugal, he could live modestly on a yearly salary of $500-$800.

Synagogues, both large and small, were able to hire a year-round cantor and often a choir to accompany him. The synagogues on the Lower East Side of New York City engaged the most recognized cantors of the period. Among them were Pinchas Minkovsky, *K'hal Adath Yeshurun* Synagogue, (Eldridge Street); Israel Cooper, Attorney Street Synagogue; Israel Michilovsky, *Beth Medrash Hagodol,* (Norfolk Street); Yechiel Karniol, *Oheb Zedek* (Norfolk Street). Permanent cantors and mixed choirs also officiated in a number of liberal temples whose membership consisted primarily of German Jews.

Although the mass European-Jewish immigration was not yet in full bloom, there were nevertheless daily arrivals. Most of the immigrants were from the *shtetl* where they had lived their entire Jewish lives in a religious atmosphere. On the first Sabbath after their arrival in America, relatives and friends would take them to the synagogue to pray and to hear the cantor. It is likely that this experience influenced many of these immigrants to remain synagogue worshippers for the rest of their lives.

During those early days, a number of prominent cantors issued a warning to their colleagues that they should unite and form an organization which would protect their welfare. Although many cantors heeded this warning and joined the organization known as *The Cantors Association of America,* it was not a professional entity. The Association was more like a

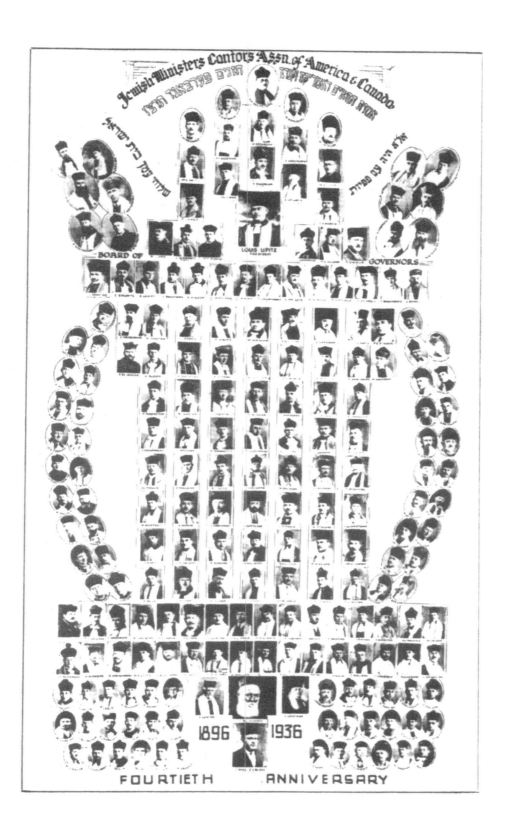

club for cantors where members would come together to discuss their profession, its difficulties and its rewards. The leadership of the organization was in the hands of cantors from synagogues established by German Jews, and the meetings were held in Germanized Yiddish, with the minutes recorded in German.

In 1903 the infamous *Kishiniv Pogrom* took place in Russia and was followed in 1905 and 1906 with similar types of attacks on Jews. The wary Jewish population began to look to emigration as the only solution, and hundreds began arriving on American shores. This immigration affected the established synagogues and especially their cantors. Orthodox synagogues began to grow in membership, and the earnest immigrants, with their strong bent towards tradition, helped develop synagogue life in America. Although immigration expanded rapidly, the European cantors were not yet willing to give up their positions in order to emigrate. Due to this unwillingness, the maturing of the American cantorate was delayed, and many cantorial positions remained vacant. In addition, as the Jewish inhabitants of the Lower East Side improved their economic situation, they found their living quarters small and cramped. They began to look for alternative housing, which they found in more upscale areas, especially Harlem and its surrounding communities.

Within a relatively short period the Jewish inhabitants began building new and often luxurious synagogues and temples. Many Gentiles felt encroached upon and moved out of their neighborhoods, leaving their churches empty. A number of these edifices were purchased and transformed into Jewish houses of worship, and the new synagogues began hiring cantors and choirs. When an adequate cantor could not be found, a well-known European *chazan* was invited. High salaries were offered, and, when American currency translated into Russian *rubles* or German *deutschmark*, it was an additional incentive to leave home and come to the *Goldene Medine* (Golden Land). This lasted until 1914.

With the outbreak of the First World War, Jews suffered terribly, especially in Russia where they became the scapegoat for the defeat of the

Czarist armies. After pogroms in the Ukraine, mass emigration took place, not only from Russia but also from many countries in Europe. Along with the new immigrants came an influx of cantors, many more than were needed. Following the war, and perhaps partially due to the war, America entered a period of prosperity, and many individuals became wealthy. Jews also found themselves in higher economic brackets and with additional wealth came the desire to build new places of worship. Synagogues costing a quarter of a million dollars and more were built with relatively small amounts of up front cash collected from the newly rich. Large mortgages and financing were secured from banking and loan institutions. How these would be repaid did not seem to present a major problem. The coming financial crisis in America and the crash on Wall Street, although lurking in some dark corner, was not yet foreseen. These newly established synagogues gobbled up the immigrant cantors; the larger the synagogue, the more prestigious the cantor desired.

Suddenly, almost overnight it seemed, the United States became the world center of cantors and cantorial art. Word spread that some *chazanim* were paid as much as $10,000 a year, and cantors began streaming into the United States from all parts of Europe. Although the situation for *star* cantors was favorable, the cantorate in general did not benefit. Each synagogue desired a *star* cantor of its own in order to compete with other synagogues. In addition, when a cantor received a decent salary, demands were made on him to be as good as, if not better than, the *star* cantors. That many *chazanim* received one-tenth the salary of the *star* cantor did not seem to enter the equation.

Gradually the new immigrant *chazanim* became members of the Jewish Ministers and Cantors Association and the leadership was taken over by the Polish and Russian cantors. Meetings were conducted in Yiddish and a determined effort to form a professional organization was undertaken. However, there were now distinct groups of cantors within the organization. The Reform cantors, who were primarily in the German-Jewish temples, were against making the organization professional. Since they were treated well, by and large, they did not feel the need for a unionized type of organization. A new group, who held positions in the recently established Conservative synagogues, also felt that they did not gain necessarily from a professional organization since their synagogues treated them relatively well. The real problems were with the largest body, the Orthodox cantors. Their plight did not seem to be of great concern to the cantors of the other movements. Along the way, three distinct organizations developed—none of them professional,— and after a number of years, the three groups amalgamated again into *The Jewish Ministers and Cantors Association* or, as it was familiarly known, the *Chazanim Farband.*

During the 1920's, the European *chazanim* kept arriving in the United States. It was a period of prosperity and synagogues hired cantors on yearly contracts. Many were supported with professional choirs conducted by first-rate musicians such as Zavel Zilberts and Meyer Machtenberg. The American Jew looked forward with great anticipation to Sabbath services in the synagogue. All week long, he worked tirelessly to provide for his family's needs. *Shabbos* was the time to forget the week day travails and to be enraptured by the improvisational artistry and *n'shomo* (soul) of the cantor. To sit in the synagogue until early afternoon was a joy. Cantorial competition, however, was very keen. Many *chazanim* were not rehired after their contracts expired and synagogue search committees set auditions, known as *probe*s, to find the next *star* cantor for their synagogue. Applicants would lead services on Sabbath without receiving compensation. A synagogue would sometimes go for months without hiring a permanent *chazan*, contenting itself with new, auditioning cantors, every week. Cantorial agents became managers and served as a liaison between cantor and synagogue. After a successful hiring and a signed contract, the managers were rewarded with a percentage of the cantor's first year salary. Often, agents would help a synagogue dismiss its cantor after the year so that they could place another *star* in his place and thus collect a percentage of the wages of the newly hired cantor.

Outside the synagogues cantors were becoming full-fledged artists for such recording companies as Columbia and RCA Victor. Cantors appeared regularly on radio programs devoted to liturgical music and Yiddish folksongs. Concert halls and Vaudeville theaters throughout North America also featured programs devoted to cantorial artistry. However, economic devastation of the Great Depression wreaked havoc with the cantorial profession. Many synagogues were forced to curtail expenditures; cantors and choirs were let go in order to relieve financial pressures, and large scale concerts were rare. During this period, new Orthodox congregations were formed, and, as these synagogues began to proliferate, they did not hire cantors but used their own members to lead services. Many began to feel that the synagogue service, with cantors singing long, intricate liturgical recitatives, was beyond the patience of the majority of the membership. The lay *baal t'fila* was, for them, a better solution. With few exceptions this has continued to be the case in the Orthodox synagogues. In Conservative and Reform synagogues, the cantor, along with the rabbi, has remained an integral part of the worship service.

THE MODERN CANTORATE

Five American institutions provide Jewish music studies and award diplomas in cantorial studies. They include The School of Sacred Music, a division of Hebrew Union College, N.Y. (Reform) established in 1948; The Cantors Institute, a division of the Jewish Theological Seminary, N.Y. (Conservative), founded in 1952; The Cantorial Training Institute of Yeshiva University (Orthodox) established in 1954. Although not separate schools for the training of cantors, there are cantorial departments in The Academy For Jewish Religion, N.Y. (Independent), and The Gratz College (Philadelphia). With the exception of the Cantorial Training Institute, the student population is comprised of both men and women. Yeshiva University offers courses in liturgical music but stresses proficiency as a *baal t'fila* rather than the professional cantor degree.

Kol b'isha erva (prohibition of women singing for men) historically prevented synagogues from allowing a woman to serve as cantor. Although a number of well known female singers were acknowledged for their cantorial ability and renditions of famous liturgical recitatives, they only performed on the concert stage but almost never as part of a religious service. Among these women were Sophie Kurzer, Bas Sheva, and Fraydele Oysher. The internationally known Malavsky Family Singers of Israel, comprised of both male and female family members, occasionally appeared in a synagogue service. They were however, sought after recording artists and appeared regularly in concerts, on radio and in films.

The *Kol B'isha* prohibition edict was side stepped by the Reform movement, and women were officially enrolled in the School of Sacred Music a short time after they were welcomed into the rabbinical school at Hebrew College Institute of Jewish Religion. The Jewish Theological Seminary followed shortly thereafter. The cantorial schools, with the exception of Yeshiva University, now regularly graduate as many women cantors as men. In several schools, female students outnumber male. In addition, many individuals, both male and female, without a degree from any of the recognized cantorial schools hold synagogue positions. They are known as Cantorial Solists and many belong to the organization, The Guild Of Temple Musicians. The full fledged cantors belong to three major organizations: The American Conference of Cantors (Reform), The Cantors Assembly of America (Conservative), The Cantorial Council of America (Orthodox). A smaller organization, The Women Cantors Network holds a conference annually and publishes newsletters several times a year. In addition, many women are also members of the Cantors Assembly and the American Conference of Cantors.

PROMINENT CANTORS OF THE "GOLDEN AGE"

ISRAEL ALTER (1901-1979) was born in L'vov and began his career as cantor at Vienna's *Briittenauer Temple-Verein* when he was twenty years old. In 1925, he moved to Hanover, Germany, where he remained for ten years before becoming cantor of the United Hebrew Congregation in South Africa. He emigrated to the United States in 1961 and became a faculty member of the School of Sacred Music, Hebrew Union College Jewish Institute of Religion. Alter made numerous recordings of songs and liturgical selections. He published his cantorial works in a collection, *Shirei Yisrael* in four volumes (1952-57). His editions of *High Holiday, Sabbath and Festivals Hazzanut* have become standards for the students of *chazanut*.

BERELE CHAGY (1892-1954) was born in Dagdo, Russia, and at age four was already helping his father, a scholar and cantor, to conduct synagogue services. With the special permission of the Lubavitcher Rebbe, he took a position with the major synagogue in Smolensk. In that city, he was the youngest cantor ever permitted to officiate at High Holiday services. After emigrating to the United States, Chagy served prominent synagogues in Detroit, Boston and Newark. In 1932, he accepted a cantorial post in Johannesburg, South Africa, and officiated there for several years. Upon returning to America, Chagy became cantor at Temple Beth El in Boro Park, Brooklyn. A lyric tenor, his "flavor" and diction were so appealing that he became one of the favorite cantors of his generation. During his lifetime, Chagy toured England, Scotland and France; he appeared in concerts at Town Hall, Carnegie Hall and Madison Square Garden in New York City.

BENZION KAPOV-KAGAN (1899-1953) sang as a boy alto and then became a traveling cantor. In 1925, he was appointed to a Rostov-Don congregation. Soon afterwards, when there was a vacancy at the famous Great Synagogue of Odessa, then the most distinguished synagogue in Russia, Kapov Kagan was chosen from among forty-two applicants. After several years, he emigrated to the United States where he officiated at the Ocean Parkway Jewish Center in Brooklyn and later at the Concourse Center of Israel in the Bronx. For a period of time he was president of the Jewish Ministers and Cantors Association. Kapov-Kagan was widely respected for his expressive interpretations, and, although others offered to write recitatives for him, he used only his own. He appeared in numerous Sunday evening concerts in the metropolitan New York area. Stricken with a serious illness at the height of his powers, he died on the second day of *Rosh Hashonah*.

ALTER YECHIEL KARNIOL (1855-1928) was invited by the Hungarian Congregation Ohab Zedek in New York City to be its cantor in 1903. He remained there for five years but then returned to Europe to officiate in the Great Synagogue of Odessa. Returning to America he became the cantor of the Rumanian Synagogue and then returned to Ohab Zedek. He had a bass voice with very high vocal range, much like a real tenor, and was an outstanding improviser. Jacob Rapaport, a recognized liturgical composer and president of the Jewish Ministers and Cantors Association, once challenged Karniol to improvise one of Rapaport's recorded selections. To the great delight of the assembled cantors, Karniol, without hesitation, created a totally new musical setting for the text. Although respected by his peers, he died in abject poverty. His grave remained without a headstone for eight years. While he was still alive, one of his admirers offered to pay for publication of his works. Karniol refused, however, and so only his recordings remain as a testament to his significance in 20th century cantorial art.

ZAVEL (ZEVULUN) KWARTIN (1874-1952) was born in Novo-Arkangelsk, Ukraine. As a young man, he studied music and sang in a synagogue choir. In 1896, on the Sabbath preceding his wedding, Kwartin officiated as *chazan* in Yelizavetgrad and thereby began his career, taking a post there that lasted until 1903. After further musical studies in Odessa and then Vienna, he officiated at Vienna's Kaiserin Elizabeth Temple. In 1908, he was appointed cantor of the Tabak Temple in Budapest, where he remained for ten years. In 1919 he emigrated to the United States and was appointed cantor of Temple Emanu-El, in Brooklyn, becoming well known for the richness and fervor of his lyric baritone voice. In 1926, Kwartin settled in Palestine where he conducted services and gave concerts. Upon his return to the United States in 1937, he accepted a cantorial position in Newark, New Jersey. He appeared on numerous recordings and his recitatives were published in 1928 as *Zemirot Zevulun*. A supplementary volume, *Tefilot Zevulun* (1938), was issued and included an autobiographical introduction. Kwartin also published his memoirs, *Mayn Leben* (1952).

SAMUEL MALAVSKY (1894-19? unverified) was born near Kiev in the Ukraine. During his youth, he sang with a number of choirs. After he came to the United States in 1914, he auditioned for Yossele Rosenblatt, and thereupon began their long association. Malavsky sang duets with Rosenblatt in concerts and on recordings, and soon was encouraged by Yossele Rosenblatt to become a cantor rather than remain only a choir singer. He officiated at several congregations and in 1947, formed the Malavsky family choir, *Singers of Israel*, with his two sons and four daughters. Although Orthodox congregations did not permit him to include his daughters in the synagogue service, the full choir did achieve international recognition with performances at public concerts and on recordings. Malavsky created a unique style for his choir, introducing an up-beat syncopation for the traditional melodies.

LEIB GLANTZ (1898-1964) was born in Kiev, Ukraine. He began his cantorial career touring Russia in the choir of his cantor father. After emigrating to the United States, Glantz took positions at various synagogues during the years 1926-43, and then settled in Tel Aviv, Israel, where he founded an academy for the training of cantors. One of the leading cantorial personalities of this era, Glantz may be considered primarily an innovator. Combining exceptional musicianship with temperament and deep understanding of the prayers, he was able to reach great heights using his unique style and original interpretations. Glantz recorded a wide range of cantorials, Yiddish and Hebrew folksongs, as well as his own arrangements of Hasidic *nigunim*. His compositions were issued in a series of volumes *Rinat Hakodesh*, published by the Tel Aviv Institute of Liturgical Music in conjunction with the Israel Music Institute.

MORDECAI HERSHMAN· (1888-1940) was born in the Ukrainian town of Chernigov. As a child, he sang with the famous cantor/composer, Zeidel Rovner. His first cantorial position was in the Choral Synagogue of Zhitomir. After only five months in that city, he was called to officiate at the Great Synagogue of Vilna where he served for seven years. Upon the suggestion of the choir leader, Leo Low, Hershman emigrated to the United States. For ten years, until his death, he served as cantor of Temple Beth-El in Boro Park, Brooklyn, During this period he also made extensive tours of Europe, South America and Palestine. Mordecai Hershman was described as more a minstrel than an officiant, whose beautiful tenor had great warmth and was of hypnotizing power. His cantorial and folk song recordings were very popular and retained their appeal late into the twentieth century. He also appeared in the 1931 film, *Voice of Israel* and may be seen on the video, *Great Cantors of the Golden Age* (Brandeis University Jewish Film Archives, 1990).

DAVID KOUSSEVITZKY (1911-1985) was born in Vilna. As a child he joined the Vilna Choir School and then later sang at the Great Synagogue of Vilna. He also studied at the Vilna Academy of Music. At the age of eighteen, he accepted the post of choir leader for the synagogue in Kremancia-Lemberg where he remained until he was conscripted into the Polish army. Upon his military discharge, Koussevitzky went to Warsaw where he studied voice. He then began officiating as guest cantor in various European cities until becoming chief cantor at the congregation in Rovno. Three years later, he accepted an invitation from the Henden Synagogue, a leading congregation in London, England. He remained there for twelve years during which time he also served as an instructor in *chazanut* at Jews College. He then emigrated to the United States and became cantor at Temple Emanuel of Boro Park, Brooklyn, where he remained until his death.

MOSHE KOUSSEVITZKY (1899-1966) was born in Smorgon, near Vilna. Early on, he possessed a graceful and powerful lyric tenor, with a particularly fine upper register. In 1924, he became cantor at the Great Synagogue of Vilna, and three years later succeeded Gershon Sirota at the Tlomacki Street Synagogue in Warsaw. At the outbreak of World War II, he escaped to Russia, where he sang concert programs in Russian, Polish and Yiddish. He also appeared in opera. In 1947, he emigrated to the United States and toured widely throughout North and South America, South Africa and Israel. In 1952, he was appointed cantor at Temple Beth-El in Boro Park, Brooklyn. Koussevitzky's many public appearances and phonograph recordings brought him considerable fame, and he was regarded as one of the great cantorial voices of his time. Most of his recordings include selections of other cantors and composers including Rosenblatt, Roitman, and Leo Low. Although he died in the United States, his burial was in Israel.

MOSHE OYSHER (1907-1958) was born in Lipkin, Bessarabia and emigrated with his family to Canada in 1921. There, he joined up with a Yiddish theatrical company and soon appeared on the Yiddish stage in New York City. He led his own company on a tour to Buenos Aires, Argentina in 1932. Returning to the United States two years later, he decided to become a *chazan* as his father and grandfather had been. Oysher conducted services in New York City and was noted for his Hasidic-like interpretations of traditional prayers. He starred in the Yiddish films, *The Cantor's Son, Yankel the Blacksmith* and *Der Vilna Balebesl*, and made numerous recordings of cantorials and Jewish folksongs. His heart may have been in the theater, but his soul remained with the synagogue. When asked to assume the leading role in a production of the *Jazz Singer*, he stipulated that he would not perform on the Sabbath.

PIERRE PINCHICK (nee Pinchas Segal, 1900-1971) was born in Zhivitov, Ukraine. As a young boy, he was sent to live with his grandfather in Podolia. While at the Yeshiva, his singing attracted the attention of one of his teachers, who arranged for him to be taught piano and voice in Rostov. Pinchick was a gifted musician who possessed a very expressive tenor. He became *chazan* in Leningrad and subsequently made his way to the United States where his talent was quickly recognized. He was famous for his originality and was known for excellent timing and exaggerated pauses employed to attract attention. He used Hasidic intonations including trills, wails, sobs, and falsetto to good advantage. In addition, he had an unusually appealing *mezzo-voce* (half-voice). *Rozo D'shabbos* is Pinchick's most acclaimed recording; the transcription was published in *The Repertoire of Pinchick*, (Cantors Assembly 1963).

DAVID ROITMAN (1884-1943) called "the poet of the pulpit" was born in the village of Derezinke, in the province of Podolia. As a young boy, he was apprenticed to Zeidel Rovner and he remained with that cantorial master throughout his teens. After serving pulpits in Vilna, St. Petersburg and Odessa, he emigrated to the United States in 1920. Following two years at Congregation Ohev Shalom of Brooklyn, Roitman accepted a position at Shaare Zedek Synagogue in Manhattan where he remained for eighteen years. Until his death in New York City, he made extensive concert tours in Europe and South America. Although widely regarded for his improvisational abilities, Roitman's recitatives actually were worked through in advance of the performance. A lyric tenor, he used a great deal of *mezzo-voce*, and demonstrated a highly developed coloratura which has been difficult to imitate. While he did not have the vocal qualities of Hershman, Rosenblatt or Kwartin, his wide use of dynamics and melodic variety nonetheless place Roitman on par with these three cantorial masters.

ARYEH LEIB RUTMAN (1866-1935) was born in Zhlobin, Russia. During his youth, he traveled throughout Russia as a choir singer. He held cantorial posts in Babroisk, Slonim, Odessa and Warsaw. Because of his growing reputation, Rutman considered a "cantor's cantor," was selected by Zanophone Records to be the first *chazan* featured on their European label. In 1913, he came to the United States on a visit and remained because of the outbreak of World War I. He served at Kehilath Jeshurun of New York, and at posts in Detroit and Boston. The eminent cantor, Samuel Joshua Weisser, reported that Rutman once sang a liturgical recitative selection by the noted synagogue composer, Eliezer Gerowitsch. Gerowitsch declared that he was awestruck because he never imagined that his music could be interpreted with such vocal artistry and temperament. Unfortunately, there are few recordings by Rutman. It was generally known that he became highly nervous during recording sessions, and none of the recordings show him at his best.

BORUCH SCHORR (1823-1904) was born in Lemberg into a prominent Hasidic family. In 1859, after officiating at various synagogues in Podolia and Rumania, he was appointed *chazan* at the great synagogue of Lemberg. As a liturgical composer, Schorr was particularly strong in terms of East European style choral music. He also wrote an operetta that was performed in the Jewish Theater of Lemberg. At the first curtain call, Schorr appeared on the stage led by the primadonna. Such public conduct was regarded by Orthodox leaders as undignified for the *chazan*, and he was suspended from his cantorial duties for a month. Hurt by this rebuke, Schorr left for New York, where he remained for five years. However, the Lemberg community recalled him to his post and he occupied that pulpit until his death. He died while officiating at services on the last day of Passover during the recitation of the words *gale k'vod malchuscho olenu* (make the glory of Your kingdom manifest upon us).

JOSEF SHLISKY (1894-1955) was born in Ostrowce, Poland. At the age of ten, he and six other boys were kidnapped by a choir leader who told their parents that he was taking them to London, but instead took them to Toronto, Canada. Shlisky managed to escape from the group, and lived with a rag dealer. When he was thirteen, he held his first cantorial position and sent for his parents as soon as he had saved enough money. Shlisky attended the Royal Conservatory of Music in Toronto, from which he graduated in 1917. Two years later he made his singing debut in New York City. For the next twenty years he held many important posts in New York, including one at the Slonimer Synagogue, and had a contract with the San Carlo Opera Company to sing leading roles in productions of La Boheme, La Juive and Tosca. A stroke tragically left him an invalid in 1940.

GERSHON SIROTA (1874-1943) was born in Podolia, Russia. At the age of twenty-one, he took his first position as *chazan* in Odessa. He then officiated in Vilna for eight years, and, in 1908, became the cantor of the Tlomackie Synagogue in Warsaw where he served for the next nineteen years. He began to make cantorial recordings as early as 1903. Esteemed as one of the most accomplished cantorial singers of his generation, Sirota possessed a dramatic tenor voice of great beauty and power, with florid coloratura and clear top notes. His perfect vocal control in all registers enabled him to produce trills of exceptional length. Writing in the British Record Collector (January 1955), critic Arthur E. Knight wrote that Sirota was "One of the most highly trained cantors of all time. His octave leaps, perfect three-note runs up the scale, fabulous trills, facile coloratura, are unrivaled by any other recording tenor. " From 1927 to 1935, he devoted his time entirely to concert tours which took him throughout Europe and the United States. Sirota was the only great cantor of his time who did not accept a position in America. In 1935, he became *chazan* at Warsaw's Norzyk Synagogue. He and his family perished in the Warsaw ghetto.

LOUIS "LEIBELE" WALDMAN (1907-1969) was born in New York City, the only American born cantor who may be considered as belonging to the great "Cantors of the Golden Age." Early recognized as a prodigy, he officiated as *chazan* and appeared in liturgical concerts while still only a youth. Waldman held positions in Boston, Mass and Passsaic NJ, and sang regularly on radio station WEVD in New York. He rapidly became quite popular for his warm lyric baritone and particularly clear diction. His flowing style was well suited to the liturgical pieces and Yiddish folksongs that he favored in concert performances and on his numerous recordings.

II

MUSIC PERSONALITIES

SALAMON SULZER 1804-1890

Salamon Sulzer is generally regarded as the father of modern *chazanut* and synagogue music. Born to a rich family of manufacturers, he became a *chazan* literally by accident. When he fell into the river as a child, and was feared drowned, his mother vowed that, if he lived, she would devote him to a sacred career. When he survived, she had the young boy study general music and *chazanut*. He excelled in his studies, and a number of years later the community of Vienna engaged him as *chazan* for its newly built temple. Sulzer possessed a phenomenal baritone-tenor and a fiery temperament to match. His appearance in Vienna caused a sensation. Instead of *chazan*, Sulzer called himself "cantor," a designation used by Johann Sebastian Bach for himself. Sulzer gave dignity to his post and demanded respect for it.

The Reform movement in Germany believed that in order to regenerate and revitalize the religious services, it was necessary to break entirely with the past and to abolish all traditional liturgy. The young Sulzer, on the other hand, believed "that the confusion of the synagogue service results from the need of only a restoration which should remain on historical grounds, and that we might find out the original noble forms to which we should anchor, developing them in artistic style."

Although Sulzer's stated purpose was to remake the traditional songs artistically, his synagogue compositions proved to be a re-shaping rather than a re-creation. He retained the traditional tunes because of the sanctity associated with them through the generations, but not as a living body filled with artistic forms. He was full of enthusiasm for Jewish ideas, and his brilliant musical renditions inflamed his listeners. His monumental *Shire Zion Vol. 1*, dedicated to the Sabbath services, was published in 1840. Twenty-seven years later *Shire Tsiyon Vol.* II, featuring compositions for the High Holidays, appeared in print.

After hearing Sulzer sing, Franz Liszt wrote

> Only once had we the opportunity to conceive what Jewish art could have been if all the intensity of the living feeling in the Jew could be expressed in forms innate of their own spirit; we met in Vienna, Cantor Sulzer. His singing of the Psalms, like the spirit of fire, soar over us to the All-high to serve as steps to His feet. The heavenly quality of his voice transports us to heaven.

As an interpreter, Sulzer grew far beyond his cantorial office. Once Franz Schubert asked him to sing his song, *Der Wanderer*, three times in succession. So moved was Schubert on hearing Sulzer that he declared "It's only now that I understand my own music and what I felt when I set the words." Schubert showed his gratitude by composing *Tov L'hodos* (Psalm 92) to the original Hebrew text. Sulzer included the composition in *Shire Zion*. Several recordings of *Tov L'hodos* have appeared and the setting remains in the repertoire of those synagogues with mixed choirs.

Sulzer's compositions are distinguished by brevity and his melodic line is always serious and dignified. Many of his melodies, especially those for the Torah Service, are standard in most Ashkenazic synagogues. In many congregations it seems almost sacreligious to omit his *En Komocho* or *Ki Mitziy*on. Furthermore, he introduced four part singing, consisting of boys (soprano and alto) and men (tenor and bass) into his temple.

Although his musical compositions were not as un-Jewish as the typical German chorales, his popularity was due primarily to his unique talent as a singer. In addition, a Sulzer mania spread among *chazanim* who began to sing, dress, and wear their hair in his style. For the first time in Jewish history, a *chazan* was honored by kings and princes, by artists and musicians.

For half a century, he was not only the "King of *Chazanim*" but he also held the veneration of the entire modern rabbinic and scholarly world. Hundreds of cantors were his students. From 1835 until 1876 practically every modern synagogue in Central Europe organized and reorganized its music according to Sulzer's service.

LOUIS LEWANDOWSKI 1821-1894

Louis Lewandowski was born in Posen, the Polish district of Germany. He received a thorough music education at the Royal Academy of Arts in Berlin becoming its first Jewish student. It was here that Lewandowski learned his technique of choral composition from the great contrapuntist, Eduard Grell. During this period, Felix Mendelssohn was approaching the acme of his fame and the young Lewandowski dreamed of becoming a second Mendelssohn. A serious nervous disorder put an end to his dreams. When he recovered, he devoted himself to the synagogue. Although he officiated as a cantor, he was primarily a choir director, a post entirely new in the history of the synagogue..

For thirty years, Lewandowski remained unnoticed as a choral leader and a singing teacher. Abraham Lichtenstein, a fine musician, became cantor of the Old Synagogue, and Lewandowski set about arranging all of his music. An apocryphal anecdote has it that the young man complained to his teacher, Grell, about the heavy burden he carried as choir director and arranger for the synagogue. Grell is said to have replied, "My dear Lewandowski, please abandon your hope to become another Mendelssohn. You are not of Mendelssohn's caliber. Rather bend your best efforts to the improvemen of your people's liturgical music."

He heeded the advice of his teacher and remained in the Old Synagogue with Lichtenstein until 1866, when both of them accepted a call to the New Synagogue, a large Reform temple with an organ. (In 1855 Lewandowski and Lichtenstein had been sent to Vienna for six months to study with Sulzer, so authoritative was Sulzer's status by that time, even in Berlin.) Now that Lewandowski had a mixed choir and organ at his disposal, many former restrictions were removed and he was able to compose at will.

For twenty-five years he worked on Lichtenstein's cantorial compositions reworking and reshaping the material. When Lewandowski published his famous *Kol Rinah Utfila*, he did not even mention Lichtenstein, believing that the music was his or had become his. The appearance of this volume in 1871 caused a sensation in cantorial circles. It was the first time that a complete service for the Sabbath and Festivals, with detailed recitatives for the entire text of the prayers, had appeared This work enabled every young man of fair musical ability and voice to master the liturgical and traditional *chazanut* in a modern form. *Kol Rina* became the most popular book for the average cantor. With the publication of his second volume, *Toda V'zimra*, Lewandowski attained the pinnacle. He became the recognized genius of synagogue song and was honored by the Jewish communities in Germany as well as by the German government, which rewarded him with medals and titles.

ABRAHAM GOLDFADEN 1840-1908

Abraham Goldfaden (Goldinfodim) was born in Volhynia, Russia. In 1857, while a student in the Rabbinical Seminary of Zhitomir, Ukraine, he was exposed to Hebrew and Yiddish literature along with liturgical chants and Jewish folksongs. This unusual seminary was a rather worldly institution with a number of teachers who were advocates of *Haskalah*, the 19th century enlightenment "Modernist" movement.

In 1877 Goldfaden founded a theater in Isai, Rumania, and toured as far as Russia with his cast made up of enthusiastic amateurs, cantors and choristers. A number of his productions, including, *Shulamith* and *Bar Kochba*, both written in operetta style, became hits with the public. When all Yiddish-language plays were banned by Russian censors, Goldfaden's flourishing theaters were forced to close. After attempting without success to produce his plays in Rumania, Galicia and Paris, Goldfaden left for the United States. On the Lower East Side of New York City he rented a hall formerly used for calisthenics which became his new theater.

Due to his lack of musical training, Goldfaden really wrote dramas interspersed with songs, arias and choruses. The orchestral accompaniments were rather primitive. He drew the tunes from the synagogue, and from Jewish, Ukrainian and Rumanian folksong. He did not shy away from employing snatches of French, Italian and Russian marches and operas. The noted musicologist, Abraham Zvi Idelsohn, catalogued 42 melodies found in *Shulamith* and *Bar Kochba* and gave "the motley origin of the music." Though Goldfaden cannot be credited with original creations of music in these two operettas, he showed a great deal of dramatic skill and musical taste in adopting fascinating tunes that appealed to the masses. Although the more developed musical taste of the post 1930's public was no longer satisfied by Goldfaden's operettas, a century ago his plays were a revelation to the people of Eastern Europe and they became sensations throughout the Jewish settlement in Russia. Apart from his dramatic creations, Goldfaden was a prolific songwriter, composing both texts and tunes. Some of his songs gained wide popularity and were published in individual sheet form, among them: *Dos Pintele Yid*, and the everlasting *Rozhinkes Mit Mandlen*, in the repertoire of Yiddish singers since 1898.

JOEL ENGEL 1868-1927

Joel Engel, distinguished teacher, critic and music authority, was born in Berdyansky, Crimea in 1868. Although his early Jewish education was weak, an interest in his heritage was piqued by a visit to Vladimir Stasov, Russia's most distinguished music critic. Their talk was joined by the famous Russian sculptor, Antokolsky, a totally assimilated Jew. Stasov took the sculptor to task for not finding the possibilites for sculpture within the life of his own Jewish people.

In an article which appeared in *The Day of New York* (Aug. 7, 1938) the distinguished composer Jacob Weinberg, records the following:

> Stasov was pacing up and down in his room. It was Easter night and as he looked out the window, Stasov exclaimed 'Behold. Soon the forty times forty churches of Moscow will resound with Easter bells. Do you know whence we got these bell-ringing? Do you know how the call was made to serve in Solomon's Temple? Through flutes and zithers and gigantic trumpets. All this comes to us from the Bible from the Holyland. How splendiferous it sounds.'

Stasov's words were a revelation for Engel, and these thoughts kindled in him the flame of nationalist creativity, a flame which illuminated his life until its very last day. That summer Engel left for the "Jewish Pale" to collect and arrange Jewish folksongs. In 1900, after three years of investigation, Engel delivered an historic lecture at the Moscow Polytechnic museum. It was a lecture which awoke in a great number of young Jewish artists a new appreciation for the attractions of Jewish life and creativity.

The *Society For Jewish Folklore* with Engel as one of its prime movers, was born, and a number of notable musicians enthusiastically flung themselves into the new movement. The society functioned from 1908 to 1918. In 1922 Joel Engel went to Berlin where he established a music publishing company, *Juval Verlag*, and issued a number of his folksong arrangements. In 1924 he resettled in Tel Aviv where he continued collecting and arranging until his death three years later. *Engel Street* was named for him in Tel Aviv.

Title page, sheet music of the *Society for Jewish Folk music*, St. Petersburg, 1911

JOSEF (YOSSELE) ROSENBLATT) 1882-1933

One need only to think of cantorial art during the 20th century and immediately the name of Yossele Rosenblatt comes to mind. No other cantor dominated cantorial music for such an extended period. Seventy years after his death Rosenblatt is still acknowledged as the master without peer. Many of his 78RPM phonograph recordings have been re-digitized, enhanced and re-mastered, and issued in audio cassettes and compact discs.

When he was seven, his father, a learned *baal t'filah*, moved the family from Southern Russia to Sadigora, Bucovina, in the Austro-Hungarian empire. Here, in a Hasidic environment, the young Yossele absorbed the plaintive wistful songs of the Hasidim along with the traditional chants of the synagogue. A child prodigy, Yossele toured Eastern Europe conducting synagogue services together with his father. At age seventeen, he officiated in the largest synagogues in Vienna while studying informally with an accomplished singer and musician. He married at eighteen and was appointed *chazan* by the community of Mukachevo.

In 1901 he served the Presburg (Bratislava) community and it was there that his fame spread throughout Europe. During this period, he continued to study and began to compose. Five years later he assumed the cantorial postion at the Orthodox congregation of Hamburg. In 1912 Rosenblatt emigrated to the United States and was elected cantor of the Hungarian *Congregation Ohab Zedek* in New York City. He soon became widely known in America and Europe through extensive concert tours and many public appearances for Liberty War Bonds.

Although he played the piano with a certain degree of proficiency, he was able to compose away from this instrument because he heard every chordal structure and harmonic progression in his head. He transcribed all his musical thoughts quickly onto paper. Jascha Zayde, the well-known pianist, said that, from a harmonic point of view, Yossele never made a mistake.

Thomas Edison, who personally recorded Rosenblatt's voice at the RCA VICTOR Studio in Camden, New Jersey, said that it was the most extraordinary range of any human voice he had ever recorded. Between 1912 and 1933 he earned several million dollars from his concert tours and recordings. With the exception of a two-year period in which he switched to Columbia records, Yossele recorded for Victor. Although there was no income tax during this period, the money did not last long because his investments and business acumen left much to be desired. His charity giving was legendary; no one was refused, neither the charitable institution nor the beggar in the subway station. Kindness, charity and gentleness were the hallmarks of his life.

Yossele sang in fifteen languages including Yiddish, Hebrew, English, Italian, French and German. He performed the *lieder* of Brahms, Beethoven, Schubert, Schuman and he loved the French and Russian repertoire which he included in his performances. In his home on 120th Street, in New York City, could be found the great singers of the age, Caruso, Ruffo, Tetrazzini, Melba and others. The Rosenblatt dining room, which could hold between 40 and 50 people, often had

Passover *Seder* guests like the Mayor of New York, and Alfred Smith, Governor of New York State. They were treated to Yossele's music as sung by the entire family. Yossele's photograph appeared whenever the Hearst newspapers featured the ten foremost Jews in America. For many, Rosenblatt was the world's best known Jew during the 1920's and early 1930's.

In 1918 Rosenblatt received an offer from Cleofonte Campanini, the director of the Chicago Opera Association, for three performances and optional performances in both New York and Boston. His salary for each performance would be $1000 plus transportation. Campaninini stipulated, "that there would be no performances on Friday or Saturday nor would Yossele have to cut or take off his beard, and there would be nothing in the performance, or his appearance upon the operatic stage that would in any way be a reflection upon the Orthodox Jewish faith...I expect Rosenblatt to make a great success in opera, as he did in his concert appearance here."

By today's economics, each performance with the Chicago Opera Company would have been worth approximately $25,000. After careful thought, Yossele decided that it was not ftting for a man of the synagogue to appear with women on stage or to be part of an operatic perfomance. It was only after a series of financial debacles, which included a Jewish newspaper and a kosher hotel in the Catskill Mountains of New York, that he was forced to "go on the road." He traveled throughout the United States and Canada, performing in vaudeville. In this medium, he did not have to appear or act with women.

Hissing and booing by the Gentile audiences on seeing him walk on stage with a large skullcap, quickly turned to great applause and "bravos" once Rosenblatt finished his first selection. He stood on the stage by himself with only a pulpit in front of him and sang cantorial compositions, opera and classic *lieder*. In 1920 during Yossele's tour of the southern United States, the great Irish tenor John McCormack was present in a Chattanooga theater audience. After the concert McCormack ran up to the stage, grasped Yossele's hand and exclaimed,

"Hello Jewish McCormack!" Rosenblatt at once repaid the tribute with, "Hello Irish Rosenblatt!" In 1921 Yossele published *Psalm 113 for Mixed Choir*, dedicated to Warren Harding. In 1928 his voice was used in the first full sound film, *The Jazz Singer*, starring Al Jolson.

In 1933 Yossele was engaged for a concert tour of Palestine. He traveled by ship and was accompanied by his son Henry who would be singing duets with his father. Yossele asked to be awakened the moment the Holy Land could be seen. At six a.m. of the last morning on board, he was awakened to catch a glimpse of Haifa and Mt. Carmel. He came on deck with tears streaming from his eyes. His wish of seeing the Holy Land would now be fulfilled. Throughout his life, he had prayed that he could live and die in the Jewish homeland. He immediately began to recite Psalms. The Israeli tour would cover the major cities in Palestine. The repertoire was to be primarily cantorial, but Yiddish and classics were also included. The accompanist was the well-known composer and pianist Nachum Nardi. Yossele performed in more than 25 concerts, but, on the night of June 18, 1933, at the age of fifty-one, he died suddenly.

YOSSELE ROSENBLATT IN SCHIRMER

In his book, *Sounds Of My Life* (New York, 1944) the noted Jewish Theater conductor/composer, Josef Rumshinsky, relates the following story. One winter's day he traveled downtown to Schirmer, at the time America's premier music company. Schirmer published and retailed some of the greatest musical works and served as a meeting place for many of the period's acclaimed musical personalities. The handpicked staff of Schirmer was of a high musical and intellectual caliber. When he entered the store, Rumshinsky saw a group of men and women listening with great concentration to the voice of Yossele Rosenblatt. He assumed that they were listening to a recording. As he drew closer, he discovered that the group was comprised of notable musicians including

Kurt Shindler, the conductor of Schola Cantorum; the symphonic composer, Professor Goldmark; and other well-known musicians. In their midst stood the diminutive Yossele singing his new composition, *Omar Rabi Elozor*. When he finished, the comments came fast and furious. "What a tremendous voice!" "Such a vocal range!" "What technique!" As an encore, Yossele gave them a demonstration of his falsetto, which he had honed to perfection. His audience was overwhelmed and almost everyone asked for his autograph. One of them, a priest, asked for an autograph but insisted that it be signed in Yiddish.

Herman Devries, the very prominent American critic of the Chicago Tribune, in his review on Cantor Rosenblatt remarked, "Rosenblatt turned handsprings of coloratura that Barrientos would very well have envied." Rosenblatt's son Henry was present in the home of Sergei Rachmaninoff, the great Russian pianist-composer. Rachmaninoff played one of his songs while the world famous basso Feodor Chaliapin sang it. The applause was deafening. The composer and artist looked at one another. Chaliapin then spoke in his thickly accented English, "If you liked that, you should have heard Rosenblatt sing it." No greater tribute could be paid to the art of Josef Rosenblatt, cantor extraordinaire, tenor without peer, artist of the first rank, and a man of whom it was said, "He was an angel walking on earth."

ERNEST BLOCH (1880-1959)

The most important Jewish composer of the twentieth century was born in Geneva, Switzerland. Although his father, a clock merchant, loved liturgical music, he wanted his son to become a merchant, not a musician. However, the young Bloch's determination to become a musician caused his father to relent. After violin studies in Geneva and Brussels, he completed courses in composition in Frankfurt, Germany. Because he failed to get a hearing on his first symphony, he returned to Geneva in 1903 and entered his father's clock business where he remained for several years, all the while composing in his spare time.

The world premiere of his *Macbeth* took place in 1910 at the *Opera-Comique* in Paris. The eminent French musicologist Romain Rolland was greatly impressed by the work and persuaded Bloch to devote himself entirely to music. Leaving the clock business, Bloch taught at the Geneva Conservatory from 1911 to 1915. He continued to compose in his spare time and began to create works more overtly Jewish in content and subject matter such as *Trois poemes juifs* ("Three Jewish Poems") for orchestra, *Israel Symphony* (inspired by the liturgy of *Yom Kippur*) and *Schelomo* ('Solomon," a rhapsodic portrait of King Solomon) for cello and orchestra.

In 1916 Bloch came to the United States and served as conductor, and teacher. In 1920 he was appointed director of the Cleveland Institute of Music. For the next ten years he composed works that were critically acclaimed including *America*. First performed in New York in 1924, his *Baal Schem* for violin has been included in the repertory of the great violinists. A grant from a wealthy San Francisco music lover enabled Bloch to retire from teaching in 1930 and devote himself to composition. He moved back to Europe and once again created a series of Jewish compositions. His most important work of this period was the *Avodath Hakodesh* ("Sacred Service") for baritone, chorus and orchestra. This Service became a classic and has been performed in liberal synagogues and concert halls in many countries.

Because of the rise of Nazism in Europe, Bloch returned to the United States in 1938. Until his retirement in 1952 he taught composition at the University of California, Berkeley.

MORDECHAI GEBIRTIG 1877-1942

Among the music treasures of every nation can be found melodies which, during the lifetime of their composer, were considered to be folk songs. While exemplifying the soul of the composer, they may also mirror the feelings and travails of an entire people. Such were the unforgettable songs of Mordechai Gebirtig, "the poet of Polish Jewry." Born in the city of Krakow, Poland, in 1877 to an impoverished home, he was forced to leave school at a young age and was apprenticed to a carpenter in order to learn a trade. He had, however, an inborn interest in music and theater and played a number of character roles in Jewish dramatic productions. In 1906, after playing the lead role in *Ghetto*, he caught the eye of the writer, Abraham Reisen, who had formed a literary group in Krakow. Under Reisen's influence, Gebirtig began writing drama criticism and, a short time later, songs.

While serving for five years in the Austrian army during World War I, he wrote songs in free moments, many of which spread quickly throughout Poland. A number of tunes such as *Kleyner Yosem* and *A Malakh Veynt*, were sung in Jewish communities world-wide. In 1920 his first book of poetry, *Folkstimlekh* (In a Folk Mode), was published in

Krakow. Songs such as *Hulyet, Hulyet Kinderlekh* and *Kinder Yorn*, became Jewish "hit" songs. The famous actress-singer, Molly Picon, among others, helped spread these songs; and the name Mordechai Gebirtig was seen regularly in most Jewish newspapers. Yiddish theaters included his *Avreml Der Marvikher, Motele, Moyshele,* and *Dos Alte Por Folk.* Special "Gebirtig Evenings" were established in Poland dedicated to the performance of his songs. In 1936 his second book, *Mayne Lider* (My Songs), containing more than fifty songs, was published in Vilna. The introduction was written by the well-known Menachem Kipnis.

In 1938 antisemitism was rampant in Poland. Gebirtig's agonizing scream, *Es Brent* (Do not stand by brothers with folded arms *watching* our town burn) was composed. The song foretold of the coming Holocaust. He sensed the end of the *Shtetl* era and of Jewish life in Poland. On June 4, 1942, Gebirtig's voice was stilled when he was shot by the Nazis as they were evacuating the Krakow Ghetto in order to send its members to the gas chambers.

92

ABRAHAM ZVI IDELSOHN 1882-1938

The "Father of Jewish music research" was born in Foelixburg, Latvia where his father served as the district *shochet* and *baal t'fila*. As a youngster, he studied in a number of *yeshivot* in Lithuania. At eighteen he began studying *chazanut*, and between 1899 and 1905 he served a number of congregations in Germany. After a short stay in Johannesburg, Idelsohn emigrated to Palestine in 1907. In Jerusalem, he discovered the great diversity of musical traditions of the Jewish people. He began to record, collect and transcribe the hundreds of melodies that were to form his monumental musicological project, the ten volume *Thesaurus of Hebrew Oriental Melodies*.

One melody heard and transcribed by Idelsohn came to represent Jewish and Israeli folksong to the world at large. Contrary to popular belief, *Hava Nagila* is not an Israeli tune but a *nigun* composed in the Hasidic court of Sadigora, Poland. Idelsohn introduced this song and offers the following information in Volume 10 of his *Thesaurus*.

This song may serve as an example of how a song becomes a popular folk song, and particualrly how a song becomes Palestinian. The tune originated in the court of Sadigora (Bukowina) and was brought to Jerusalem. In 1915, I wrote it down. In 1918, I needed a popular tune for a performance of a mixed choir in Jerusalem. My choice fell upon this tune which I aranged in four parts and for which I wrote Hebrew text. The choir sang it and apparently caught the imagination of the people, for the next day men and women were singing the song throughout Jerusalem. In no time, it spread throughout the country, and thence throughout the Jewish world. I printed the song, in my arrangement, in my Hebrew songbook *Sefer Hashirim*, page 164-165. Since then it has been printed in several songsters as Palestinian.

Idelsohn earned his livelihood as a grade school teacher and served as a lecturer in teachers' seminaries. In addition, he was also active in the cultural life of the Jewish community. By 1921, research had become his main occupation. Due to declining health and the post-World War I economic depression in the Holy Land, he left for Berlin where he remained a year, arranging for the publication of his *Thesaurus* and the songbooks that he had compiled in Jerusalem. In the winter of 1923, he came to the United States and was invited by Hebrew Union College in Cincinnati to catalog the *Edward Birnbaum Collection* one of the most extensive and important Jewish music collections in Europe.

JAN PEERCE (1904-1984)

Jan Peerce was born Jacob Pincus Perelmuth on June 3, 1904, in New York City to Russian Jewish immigrants. As a child, he sang in local synagogue choirs and studied the violin. Not long after his bar mitzvah, his parents opened Green Mansion, a catering hall for wedding receptions. The young Perelmuth formed his own music group, called *Pinky Pearl and His Society Dance Band,* and performed for a fee at the weddings. In 1918, he performed with his group in the Borscht Belt (Catskill Mountains resorts) and continued in various theaters, cabarets and dance halls through the early 1930s. In 1932, the impresario Samuel L. ("Roxy") Rothafel convinced him to give up the violin and study voice. After changing his name first to John Pierce and then to Jan Peerce, Rothafel also arranged for him to join the Radio City Music Hall and the *Radio City Music Hall of the Air* radio program.

Throughout the 1930's Peerce performed regularly at the Radio City Music Hall and the Paramount Theater in New York City. On the *Forverts* (Forward) radio program he sang Yiddish, Hebrew and cantorial music under the name Jascha Pearl. In 1938 Peerce sang the first act of Wagner's *Die Walkure* in the *Radio City Music Hall of the Air* The famed conductor, Arturo Toscanini, heard the performance and hired Peerce to sing the tenor solo in a radio broadcast of Beethoven's Ninth Symphony. Over the next fifteen years, Peerce and Toscanini worked together many times.

In 1941 Peerce joined the Metropolitan Opera Company and remained there for the next twenty-five years achieving world wide acclaim. He retired from the Met during the 1967-1968 season but continued to give recitals and concerts with major orchestras. In 1971 he appeared on Broadway as Tevye in *Fiddler on the Roof*.

Peerce made a series of recordings of Yiddish folk songs and liturgical masterpieces for RCA Victor and the Vanguard Recording Society. These recordings include *Jan Peerce Sings Hebrew Melodies*, *Jan Peerce On 2nd Avenue*, *Yiddish Folk Songs*, *Fiddler On The Roof* and *Jewish Folk Songs*, *The Yiddish Dream*, *The Art of the Cantor*, and *Cantorial Masterpieces*. Two years before his death he appeared in Dayton, Ohio, as distinguished soloist in a concert of liturgical compositions featuring the Beth Abraham Youth Chorale. *Jan Peerce, The Final Recording* was issued shortly before he passed away.

RICHARD TUCKER 1913-1975

Richard Tucker (nee Rubin Ticker) was born in New York City. He learned traditional Jewish melodies at home from his Orthodox father, an immigrant from Eastern Europe. From age six through thirteen Rubin sang as a boy alto in the choir of the prominent cantor, Samuel Weisser, with whom he also studied cantorial singing. Later he was tutored by the well-known choir leader and liturgical composer, Zavel Zilberts.

In 1934 he married Sara Perelmuth, sister of Jan Peerce. At the time, he was a fur salesman and a part-time cantor at Temple Emanuel in Passaic, New Jersey. He changed his name to Richard Tucker in 1937, and became the full cantor at Adath Israel Synagogue in the Bronx, New York, the following year In 1943 he accepted the cantorial position at the prestigious Brooklyn Jewish Center where he worked closely with Sholom Secunda the famed choir leader and music director.

In 1944 Tucker was signed by the Metropolitan Opera. For the next thirty-one years, Tucker made numerous appearances at the Metropolitan Opera in New York City and in opera houses and concert halls throughout America, Europe and Israel. Several years after World War II, Tucker conducted Sabbath services in the

Vienna synagogue which Sulzer had made famous in the 19th century. Tucker regarded this service as his greatest single performance. On the eve of the Six Day War in 1967, Tucker broke down with emotion on an Israeli stage. Although he wanted to be with his fellow Jews during the coming conflict, he along with other visiting artists, was advised to leave.

In addition to his numerous operatic recordings, Tucker also made a number of cantorial, Israeli and Yiddish recordings which affected generations of cantors and Jewish singers. His recordings include: *Welcoming The Sabbath*, *Kol Nidre*, *Cantorial Pearls*, *A Passover Seder Festival*, and *Rozhinkes Mit Mandlen* (featuring a selection of songs by Abraham Goldfaden). It is reported that Elvis Presley was strongly influenced by repeatedly listening to Tucker's cantorial music.

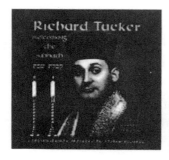

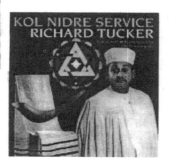

LEONARD BERNSTEIN 1918-1990

Leonard Bernstein was born in Lawrence Massachusetts. After graduating from Harvard University in 1939 he studied piano, conducting, and orchestration at the Curtis Institute of Music in Philadelphia. In Tanglewood, Bernstein became the conducting assistant to Serge Koussevitsky, the famous conductor of the Boston Symphony Orchestra. On November 14, 1943, Bernstein substituted on a few hours notice for the ailing Bruno Walter at a Carnegie Hall concert. The program was broadcast nationally on radio to critical acclaim and soon orchestras worldwide sought him out as a guest conductor.

In 1947 he conducted the Israel Philharmonic Orchestra in Tel Aviv, beginning a relationship that lasted until his death. After years of conducting and teaching in Tanglewood and Brandeis University, Bernstein became the Music Director of the New York Philharmonic Orchestra in 1958, a post he held until 1969. More than half of Bernstein's 400 recordings were made with the New York Philharmonic Orchestra.

Inspired by his Jewish heritage, Bernstein completed his first large-scale work, Symphony No 1: Jeremiah (1943). His Symphony No. 3: "Kaddish," composed in 1963, was premiered by the Israel Philharmonic Orchestra. "Chichester Psalms" for chorus, boy soprano and orchestra was premiered in 1965. "The Dybbuk Variations" (1974) is a ballet based on a Yiddish play by S. Ansky about exorcism in a Hasidic community in eastern Europe. "Halil" ("Flute," 1981) is for flute, string orchestra, and percussion, and is dedicated to the memory of an Israeli soldier killed in action.

SHLOMO CARLEBACH 1926-1994

Rabbi Shlomo Carlebach was born in Berlin, Germany to a noted rabbinical dynasty. When the family emigrated to the United States, Shlomo studied in several prominent yeshivot including advanced studies at the *Bais Medrash Elyon* in Monsey, New York. Acknowledged as an *iluyi* (genius) in Talmudic knowledge, he was also blessed with a photographic memory. In the 1950's he began his outreach work with uncommitted Jews, a labor which lasted throughout his lifetime.

During the early 1960's when most of the Jewish recordings available in the United States were by the great "star" cantors or members of the Yiddish Theater on Second Avenue in New York City, Shlomo Carlebach issued his first recording, *Hanshomo Loch* (My Soul Belongs To You). The melodies, the musical arrangements by Milt Okun (arranger for Harry Belafonte and other great American recording artists) and the sound of the music made many Jewish listeners wince on first hearing. The Eastern European style so prevalent in much of Jewish music heretofore, was hardly to be found. The minor mode to which most Ashkenazic Jews had become accustomed, was not always evident. In its place were a different set of sounds, Jewish tones mixed with American tones. Nevertheless, the sounds of *Eso Enai* and *Hanshomo Loch* found favor in the American Jewish ear and his songs soon became a permanent part of the Jewish "folk" repertoire. His melodies were so widely known that they were sometimes inaccurately given historical longevity. In addition, they were often incorrectly attributed to other composers and Hasidic groups.

For the last third of the 20th century, Shlomo had the distinction of being one of the few American Jewish composers whose songs were regularly performed by Israeli artists on radio, television, and concerts. The *Rabi Haroked* (the Dancing Rabbi), as he was affectionately known throughout Israel, composed such songs as *V'haer Enenu, Od Yishama, Adir Hu, Uvau Ha'ovdim, Yisrael B'tach Bashem, L'ma'an Achai V'reai* and hundreds of others. They remain part of the Jewish song repertoire. His *Am Yisrael Chai* became the unofficial hymn of the "Student Struggle for Soviet Jewry." His melodies served as the cornerstone for music in the Modern Orthodox and right wing Orthodox yeshivas as well as the most left wing congregational Hebrew schools. His songs were sung with exuberant joy in the Orthodox, Conservative and Reform summer camps. Most wedding and Bar Mitzvah bands continue to pay homage to Carlebach by playing sets of his melodies at traditional Jewish affairs. His musical legacy lives on with the proliferation of *Carlebach Services*, sometimes referred to as *Happy Minyans* in Israel, North America, Europe, Australia, and South America.

Esa Énai

S. Carlebach

Moderately

E-sa é-nai el_ he-ha-rim mé-a-yin mé-a-yin

ya-vo ez-ri ya-vo ez-ri ez - ri

me-im Ha-shem o - sé sha-ma-yim va-a-rets

E-sa é-nai el he-ha-rim
Mé-a-yin ya-vo ez-ri
Ez-ri me-im Ha-shem
O-sé sha-ma-vim va-a-rets

אֶשָּׂא עֵינַי אֶל הֶהָרִים
מֵאַיִן יָבוֹא עֶזְרִי
עֶזְרִי מֵעִים יְיָ
עוֹשֵׂה שָׁמַיִם וָאָרֶץ

I lift up my eyes to the hills. Whence comes my help? My help is
from the Lord, Creator of heaven and earth.

Esa Enai is one of Rabbi Shlomo Carlebach's signature melodies. Featured on his first
long-playing phonograph recording, *Hanshomo Loch*, it has remained popular into
the 21st century

ITZHAK PERLMAN 1945-

Itzhak Perlman was born in Israel to parents who had migrated from Poland in the mid-1930's. Stricken with polio at the age of four, he was left permanently deprived of the use of his legs. He has always played seated. At age thirteen, he appeared twice on the Ed Sullivan TV show to great critical acclaim. Scholarships to the Juilliard School of Music followed, and Perlman was able to study with outstanding, master violin teachers.

His official concert debut took place in a Carnegie Hall performance in 1963. During the 1965-66 season he made his first major American tour performing from coast to coast. Since the mid 1970's he has toured extensively, performing throughout the world giving about one hundred concerts a year. For many years Perlman was a member of a musical circle and performed with some of its members, including Vladimir Ashkenazy, Pinchas Zukerman, Isaac Stern, Daniel Barenboim and Zubin Mehta. Perlman appeared often in Israel, especially with the Israel Philharmonic Orchestra.

One of the most recorded classical violinists of the 20th century, Perlman also recorded three hugely successful recordings of Yiddish music. In *Tradition* Perlman plays popular Jewish melodies accomp-anied by the Israel Philharmonic Orchestra. In successive recordings, *In the Fiddler's House*, and *Live in the Fiddlers House*, Perlman rediscovered his Klezmer roots with the help of four top Klezmer groups: *The Klezmer Conservatory Band*, *Brave Old World*, The *Klezmatics* and *Andy Statman*. A sold-out *Fiddler's House* national tour followed.

GIORA FEIDMAN 1936-

Giora Feidman is acclaimed as one of the great virtuoso clarinetists of our time. As an essentially Jewish musician, his influence has been felt far beyond the Klezmer music which has become his personal signature. A protagonist of contemporary Jewish cross-over music, he demonstrates a musical understanding that defies any attempt to be categorized.

Born in 1936 to Jewish immigrants in Buenos Aires, Argentina, it was soon evident that the young Giora was to continue in the tradition of a family renowned for four generations of Klezmer musicians. He received a classical music education, and at eighteen was appointed soloist at the famous Teatro Colon in Buenos Aires. At the age of twenty he became the youngest solo wind player with the Israel Philharmonic Orchestra where he remained for two decades under the baton of the world's great conductors.

In the early 1970's Giora Feidman launched his mission to bring the heritage of Jewish music to the world stage. Thus the renaissance of Klezmer began, and is now accepted as an integral part of world music. His repertoire continued to expand. He was determined to bring the so called "folk music" to the classical concert hall. (It is to his credit that both chamber and symphonic music have been composed based on traditional Jewish folk and liturgical elements.)

In addition to making numerous recordings, Feidman has appeared in concert halls, opera stages and theaters and film. His clarinet playing can be heard in the Oscar winning film *Schindler's List*.

Recordings

Sheet Music

DEBBIE FRIEDMAN 1951-

The leading contemporary Jewish songwriter/vocalist is a native of Minnesota. After serving as a cantor for a number of years, she devoted herself completely to writing and performing. Her music is widely sung in liberal synagogues, schools, camps and community centers throughout North America. American popular music artists of the 1960's and 1970's including, Peter Paul and Mary, Joan Baez, Judy Collins and Melissa Manchester originally influenced Friedman. She has performed in hundreds of cities in the United States, Canada, Europe and Israel and performs regularly for Jewish organizations, conferences, and community centers. She has also directed music and singing programs at major university campuses. Many of her melodies have become the hallmark of "Renewal" and "Healing" services, and her best-known *Mishebeirach* brings respite and hope into countless lonely hospital rooms and rehabilitation centers. Her 17 recordings have been a powerful influence on younger contemporary singers and songwriters who have emulated and adapted her style. Debbie's Carnegie Hall concert marked the 25th anniversary of the beginning of her musical career. Her recordings include: *And You Shall Be A Blessing*, *Live At The Dell*, *In the Beginning*, *World of Your Dreams*, and *Water in the Well* and *Shirim al Galgalim*.

III

FROM THE REPERTOIRE

Z'MIROT

Zmirot in the home can be traced back to two traditions originating in Talmudic times. According to the first, two angels escort the Jew on the eve of the Sabbath as he makes his way home from the synagogue. The *Zohar*, the book of Kabalist thought, expanded this idea until all domestic activities of the Sabbath were supposed to be under heavenly guardianship, especially the three Sabbath meals. According to the second tradition, the Sabbath is to be distinguished and solemnized by extraordinary food and drink. In exalting the Sabbath over the ordinary days of the week, the Jew imitates the Lord himself who rested on the Sabbath from his labors of Creation. Most of the poetic thoughts that permeate the *Z'mirot* are based on, or derived from, these main ideas.

The word *Z'mirot* means "hymns" or "songs." Among the Sephardim, *Z'mirot* refers to the Biblical verses and Psalms recited in the preliminary Sabbath morning service known as *P'suke D'zimra*. In *Ashkenaz* tradition, the term refers to *Z'mirot shel Shabbat*, translated variously as table songs, domestic songs and home songs. *Z'mirot shel Shabbat* in the home, were also part of the Sephardic tradition where they were known as *pizmonim*. Beginning with Dunash ben Labrat in the 10th century, and culminating with Rabbi Isaac Luria (1534-1572), known as the *Ari*, many poets wrote poems glorifying the Sabbath. These poems, later inserted into the *Siddur* (the prayerbook), became popular as *Z'mirot* which were sung at the *Shalosh S'udos* (the three Sabbath meals—Friday evening, Sabbath noon, Sabbath afternoon) and the *Melave Malka* (the evening celebratory meal following the Sabbath). Just as the Sabbath is central to Jewish life and tradition, its music was always indispensable in reinforcing the joy and holiness of the day. The singing of *Z'mirot* was a firmly rooted custom in virtually all lands where Jews settled and was already an established practice in the early Middle Ages.

Among the most popular *Z'mirot* are *Kol M'kadesh Sh'vi'i, Ya Ribon, Tsur Mishelo Achalnu*, and *Yom Ze M'chubad. Ma Yofis*, a *Z'mira* which had once been well known, lost much of its popularity due to its tragic association. The tune, probably German in origin, gained popularity in Poland among Gentiles as well as Jews. Often during drunken revelries, Polish gentry forced "their Jews" to play the buffoon and entertain them by mimicking and parodying liturgical songs. The singing and mimicking of *Ma Yofis* was an integral part of this drunken activity. Sadly, it was known that some Jews, wishing to ingratiate themselves with the Gentile Lords, allowed themselves to be mocked and debased. The term *Ma Yofis Jew*, came to imply servility and self-deprecation. The epithet *mayofisnik*, is defined in modern Yiddish dictionaries as a servile Jew.

M'nucha V'simcha

M'nu-cho v'-sim-cho or la'y'-hu-dim
Yom sha-ba-ton yom ma-cha-ma-dim
Shom-rav v'-zoch-rav hé-ma m'-l-dim
Ki l'-shi-sha kol b'-ru-im v'-om-dim

מְנוּחָה וְשִׂמְחָה
אוֹר לַיְּהוּדִים
יוֹם שַׁבָּתוֹן יוֹם מַחֲמַדִּים
שׁוֹמְרָיו וְזוֹכְרָיו הֵמָּה מְעִידִים
כִּי לְשִׁשָּׁה כָּל בְּרוּאִים וְעוֹמְדִים.

Rest and contentment, joy and light are in store for
Jews on this Sabbath day-the day of delights

Shalom Aléchem

Sha-lom a-lé-chem mal-a-ché ha-sha-rét mal-a-ché el-yon
Mi-me-lech mal-ché ham-la-chim ha-ka-dosh baruch hu
Bo-a-chem l'-sha-lom mal-a-ché ha-shalom mal-a-ché el-yon
Mi-me-lech mal-ché ham-la-chim ha-ka-dosh ba-ruch hu
Bar-chu-ni l'-shal-om mal-a-ché ha-shalom mal-a-ché el-yon
Mi-me-lech mal-ché ham-la-chim ha-ka-dosh ba-ruch hu
Tsét-chem l'-sha-lom mal-a-ché ha-shalom mal-a-ché el-yon
Mi-me-lech mal-ché ham-la-chim ha-ka-dosh ba-ruch hu

שָׁלוֹם עֲלֵיכֶם מַלְאֲכֵי הַשָּׁרֵת מַלְאֲכֵי עֶלְיוֹן
מִמֶּלֶךְ מַלְכֵי הַמְּלָכִים הַקָּדוֹשׁ בָּרוּךְ הוּא
בּוֹאֲכֶם לְשָׁלוֹם מַלְאֲכֵי הַשָּׁלוֹם מַלְאֲכֵי עֶלְיוֹן
מִמֶּלֶךְ מַלְכֵי הַמְּלָכִים הַקָּדוֹשׁ בָּרוּךְ הוּא
בָּרְכוּנִי לְשָׁלוֹם מַלְאֲכֵי הַשָּׁלוֹם מַלְאֲכֵי עֶלְיוֹן
מִמֶּלֶךְ מַלְכֵי הַמְּלָכִים הַקָּדוֹשׁ בָּרוּךְ הוּא
צֵאתְכֶם לְשָׁלוֹם מַלְאֲכֵי הַשָּׁלוֹם מַלְאֲכֵי עֶלְיוֹן
מִמֶּלֶךְ מַלְכֵי הַמְּלָכִים הַקָּדוֹשׁ בָּרוּךְ הוּא

Peace be upon you, angels of the Exalted One, from the King, the Holy One blessed be He. May your coming be for the sake of peace. Bless me for peace; and may your departure as well be with peace.

Rabbi Israel Goldfarb's melody for *Shalom Aléchem* is the standard in most Jewish communities world-wide. In addition to the text of *Shalom Aléchem*, the melody is often used for other texts in the liturgy. In many congregations it has been adapted to *v'énénu tirena* in the *K'dusha* of the Sabbath and festival *Shacharit* service.

Ya Ribon

Ya ri-bon a-lam v'-al-ma-ya

Ant hu mal-ka me-lech mal-cha-ya

O-vad g'-vur-téch v'-tim-ha-ya

Sh'-far ko-da-mach l'-ha-cha-va-ya

יָהּ רִבּוֹן עָלַם וְעָלְמַיָּה

אַנְתְּ הוּא מַלְכָּא מֶלֶךְ מַלְכַיָּה

עוֹבַד גְּבוּרְתֵּךְ וְתִמְהַיָּה

שְׁפַר קָדָמָךְ לְהַחֲוַיָּא

Master of the world and of all worlds, You are the King who reigns over all kings. It is wonderful to declare your powerful deeds.

Ma Y'didut

Ma y'-di-dut m'nu-cha-téch	מַה יְּדִידוּת מְנוּחָתֵךְ
At Sha-bat ha-mal-ka	אַתְּ שַׁבָּת הַמַּלְכָּה
B'chén narutz lik-ra-téch	בְּכֵן נָרוּץ לִקְרָאתֵךְ
Bo-i ka-la n'-su-cha	בּוֹאִי כַלָּה נְסוּכָה
L'vush big-dé cha-mu-dot	לְבוּשׁ בִּגְדֵי חֲמוּדוֹת
L'had-lik nér biv-ra-cha	לְהַדְלִיק נֵר בִּבְרָכָה
Va-té-chel kol ha-a-vo-dot	וַתֵּכֶל כָּל הָעֲבוֹדוֹת
Lo ta-a-su m'la-cha	לֹא תַעֲשׂוּ מְלָאכָה.
L'hit-a-nég b'-ta-a-nu-gim	לְהִתְעַנֵּג בְּתַעֲנוּגִים
Bar-bu-rim us-lav v'da-gim	בַּרְבּוּרִים וּשְׂלָיו וְדָגִים.

How beloved is your rest, Sabbath Queen! Therefore we run to welcome you. The flames are kindled, and all labor ceases.

Yom Ze L'yisraél

Sephardic Folktune

Yom ze l'-yis-rá-él	יוֹם זֶה לְיִשְׂרָאֵל
O-ra v'-sim-cha	אוֹרָה וְשִׂמְחָה
Sha-bat m'-nu-cha	שַׁבָּת מְנוּחָה

This day is for Israel—a day of light and gladness, the Sabbath of rest.

Tsur Mishelo

Tsur mi-she-lo a-chal-nu
Ba-r'-chu e-mu-nai
Sa-va-nu v'-ho-tar-nu
Kid-var A-do-nai

צוּר מִשֶּׁלוֹ אָכַלְנוּ
בָּרְכוּ אֱמוּנַי
שָׂבַעְנוּ וְהוֹתַרְנוּ
כִּדְבַר יְיָ

Let us bless the Lord whose food we ate. Let us thank Him with our lips, chanting; There is no one holy like our Lord.

LADINO FOLK SONGS

From Roman times until 1492 there had been a strong Jewish presence in the Iberian Peninsula. Although Jewish balladeers, minstrels and dancers had participated in the wedding celebrations of Ferdinand of Aaragon and Isabella of Castille (1469), progroms had already started in 1391 with the destruction of the Jewish community in Seville. Over the next decade the pogroms spread to Cordova, Toledo, Barcelona, Catalonia and Valencia. Soon there were *conversos* (converts) or *marranos*, a term for Jews who felt compelled to convert publicly to Christianity. During the Inquisition, the Spanish word *marrano* meaning "pig," became a pejorative epithet for any Jews converted to Christianity. The general belief at the time was that these converts still secretly observed Judaism, including the Jewish dietary laws, and abstained from eating pork.

Despite the vicissitudes of life in those times, Jews flourished in Spain in what they considered to be a "golden age" of cultural enrichment and intellectual achievement, a great era of Sephardic (Judeo-Spanish) civilization. When Ferdinad and Isabella mercilessly banished the Jewish minority which refused to convert to Catholicism, a unique pattern of cultural survival was set in motion. More than 170,000 Sephardim are believed to have left Spain after March 31, 1492, to wander throughout the Mediterranean in search of a hospitable refuge. Although some drifted as far north as London, Amsterdam, Vienna and Hamburg, the majority settled in various parts of the Ottoman Empire and formed enclaves in such large metropolitan centers as Alexandria, Cairo, Adrianople, Constantinople, Jerusalem and Salonika, where the Sephardic Jews had their largest community until World War II.

The sultans were liberal in their attitude towards the newcomers. They were free to worship as they pleased, use their own language, maintain their own schools and community services, and engage in professions and commerce. In these large and prosperous open ghettos, the old Spanish dress, customs, food and folk culture were retained. The

Jews continued to speak the language of their former homeland and to sing the songs of the Spanish troubadours. They wrote Ladino in *Rashi* script and those who did not speak it named their dialect *Judesmo*. These Spanish Jews never for a moment doubted that their language, songs and folk culture were Jewish, though it was in fact pure Castillian in origin. By the twentieth century, many foreign elements had crept into the language of the exiles because of their lengthy stay and acculturation in the new host countries. In present day Ladino, one may find Turkish, French, Greek and Slavic words, together with many of the same words for religious ideas and customs that are currently found in Yiddish.

Ladino may be characterized as "frozen" archaic Spanish. It was a dialect spoken wherever colonies of Sephardim, Spanish Jews formed after their expulsion in 1492, in the Balkans, North Africa, Central and South America and in parts of the United States. According to some scholars, certain aspects of Ladino are even more archaic than the Castilian Spanish spoken in 1492. Because Jews were confined to *aljamos* (Jewish quarters) during their centuries of living in Spain, the older pronunciation persisted. Their ballads and folk songs, too, go back to medieval times.

Following the Expulsion, the Judeo-Spanish folk songs developed in two directions: ballads inspired by the Bible, the Patriarchs, religious holidays, Commandments, moral values; and songs of love and the human life cycle. The widely scattered Jews seemed to have absorbed new melodies from the host cultures and used them for the old ballads. It therefore seems unlikely that the original melodies can be reconstructed by studying performance of Sephardic Jews. Far away from their country of origin, creative Jews were inevitably influenced by their new surroundings in the countries of exile.

Researchers have shown that during the first part of the eighteenth century, the musical repertoire of the Balkan and eastern Mediterranean Jewish communities gradually diverged from that of the Jews of Morocco, who maintained closer contact with Spain. Over the years, the rich folk content of their songs underwent subtle changes. However, it is quite probable that, despite changes, the contemporary musical repertoire of the ballads can be considered essentially a direct offspring of the *romanceros* created in Spain before the Expulsion. Many passages expressing old prejudices and foreign beliefs were deleted, and verses conforming better to Jewish ideals were substituted. It was the women who were responsible for the survival of the Ladino folk songs. Mothers taught them to their children at an early age. It was to be expected that the music, while originally strongly Spanish in character, often shows a pronounced Greco-Turkish strain. Nevertheless, there is also frequently a similarity to East European folk songs or synagogue chants.

Cuando El Rey Nimrod

Spirited

Cuan - do el rey Nim - rod al cam - po sa - li - a mi -
ra - va en el cie - lo y en la es - tre - ye - ri - a vi - do u - na luz san - ta
en la giu - de - ri - a que ha - vi - a de na - cer
Av - ra - ham a - vi - nu Av - ram a - vi - nu pa - dre que - ri -
do pa - dre ben - di - cho luz de Is - ra - él luz de Is - ra - él

Cuando el rey Nimrod al campo salia	When King Nimrod went out into the fields
Mirava en el cielo y en la estreyeria	He looked at the heavens and at all the stars
Vido una luz santa en la giuderia	He saw a holy light above the Jewish quarter
Que havia de nacer *Avraham avinu*	A sign that Abraham our father was about to be born
Avraham avinu padre querido	Abraham our father, beloved father
Padre bendicho luz de *Israel*	Blessed father, light of Israel
Saludemos al compadre y tambien al *moel*	Let us greet the godfather and also the mohel
Que por su *z'chut* mos venga el *goel*	Because of his virtue may the Messiah come
Y ri'hma a todo *Israel*	To redeem all Israel
Cierto loaremos al verdadero	Surely we will praise the true redeemer
Al verdadero de *Israel*	The true redeemer of Israel

Cuando El Rey Nimrod, one of the most famous Ladiono songs, is also sung in many Sephardic communities to the Sabbath text *Shalom Aléchem*.

Los Bilbilicos

Moderately

Los bil - bi - li - cos___ can - tan con sos -
pi - ros de___ a - mor los mor mi ne - sha - ma s'es___ cu -
re_____ se su___ frien - do del___ a - mor_____ mi ne -
sha - ma y___ mi ven - tu - ra es - ta en_____ tu__ po - der___

Los bilbilicos cantan	The nightingales sing
Con sospiros de amor	With sighs of love
Mi neshama mi ventura	My soul and my fate
Estan en tu poder	Are in your power
La rosa enflorese	The rose blooms
En el mes de mai	In the month of May
Mi neshama s'escurese	My soul and my fate
Sufriendo del amor	Suffer from love's pain
Mas presto ven palomba	Come more quickly dove
Mas presto ven con mi	More quickly come with me
Mas presto ven querida	More quickly come beloved
Corre y salvame	Run and save me

This Ladino song also known by the title *La Rosa Enflorese*, is common to many Sephardic communities. It was also adapted to the liturgical *Z'mira* text, *Tsur Mishelo Achalnu* and is sung in the home during the first Sabbath meal on Friday night.

Adiyo Kerida

Music and Lyrics
Traditional

Tu madre kuando te pario
I te kito al mun-do
Ko-ra-son e-ya no-te dio
Pa-ra a-mar se-gun-do
mar se-gun-do____
A-di-yo____ a-di-yo ke-ri-da____ no ke-ro la-vi-da____
Me l'am-ar-ga-tes tu____ a-tu

Tu madre kuando te parlo	When your mother bore you
I te kito al mundo	And brought you into the world
Korason eya no te dío	She gave you no heart
Para amar segundo	To love another
Adiyo, adiyo kerida	Farewell, farewell beloved
No kero la vida	I no longer wish to live
Me l'amargates tu	You made life bitter for me
Va bushkate otra amor	Go and look for another love
Aharva otras puertas	Knock on other doors
Aspera otra ardor	Wait for other ardor
Ke para mi sos muerta	Because for me you are dead

This was one of the most beloved songs in the Balkan countries during the mid 20th century.
Verdi incorporated the melody, with changed rhythm, into *la Traviata*

Non Komo Muestro Dyo

Allegretto

1. Én ke-lo-hé-nu, én ka-do-né-nu, én k'-mal-ké-nu, én k'-mo-shi-é-nu

Non komo muestro Dyo, non komo muestro Sinyor

Non komo muestro Re, non komo muestro Salvador

2. Mi che-lo-hé-nu, mi cha-do-né-nu, mi ch'-mal-ké-nu, mi ch'-mo-shi-é-nu

Ken komo muestro Dyo, ken komo muestro Sinyor

Ken komo muestro Re, ken komo muestro Salvador

3. No-de lé-lo-hé-nu, no-de la-do-né-nu no-de l'-mal-ké-nu, no-de l'-mo-shi-é-nu

Loaremos a muestro Dyo, loaremos a muestro Sinyor

Loaremos a muestro Re, loaremos a muestro Salvador

4. Baruch E-lo-hé-nu, ba-ruch A-do-né-nu, ba-ruch mal-ké-nu, ba-ruch Mo-shi-é-nu

Bendicho muestro Dyo, bendicho muestro Sinyor

Bendicho muestro Re, bendicho muestro Salvador

5. A-ta hu E-lo-hé-nu, a-ta hu A-do-né-nu, ata hu Mal-ké-nu, a-ta hu Mo-shi-é-nu

Tu el muestro Dyo, Tu el muestro Salvador

The traditional *En Kelohenu* combined with the Ladino translation
is sung in many Sephardic communities.

Ocho Kandelikas

Moderately

Flory Jagoda

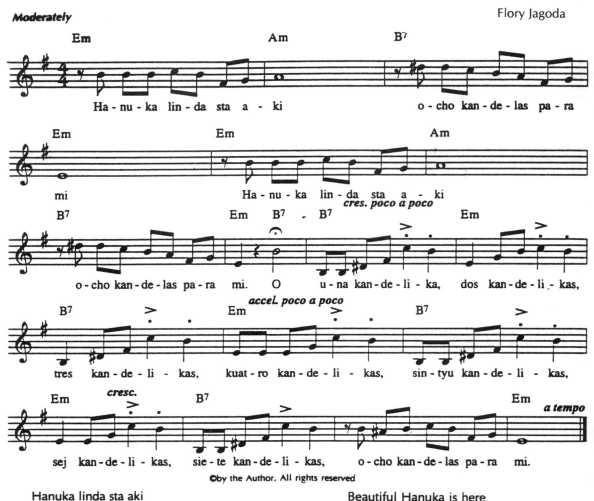

Hanuka linda sta aki	Beautiful Hanuka is here
Ocho kandelas para mi O	Eight candles for me O....
Refrain	Refrain
Una kandelika, dos kandelikas	One candle, two candles
Tres kandelikas, kuatro kandelikas	Three candles, four candles
Sintyu kandelikas, sej kandelikas	Five candles, six candles
Siete kandelikas	Seven candles
Ocho kandelas para mi	Eight candles for me
Muchas fiestas vo fazer	Many parties I will have
Kon alegriyas i plazer O.... *Refrain*	With happiness and pleasure O... Refrain
Los pastelikos vo kumer	The little pastries we will eat
Kon almendrikas i la myel O... *Refrain*	Filled with almonds and honey O...Refrain

In Yugoslavia, on each of the eight nights of Hanuka, "matchmaking parties" were held, and, while the young people sang and danced, their parents and grandparents enjoyed planning their children's weddings. Little almond cakes were eaten to assure luck, happiness, and prosperity.

HASIDIC SONG

The Hasidic movement originated in the Middle 1700's and spread throughout eastern Europe. By the end of the 19[h] century its adherents numbered between three and four million. Rabbi Israel, the founder of this movement, who became known as the *Baal Shem Tov* (master of the Good Name), felt that Jewish religious observance had become a joyless and arid habit rather than a daily rejuvenating experience. "Worship the Lord with joy, come before Him with song," said the Psalmist. Rabbi Israel preached that the simple man, imbued with native faith and able to pray fervently and wholeheartedly with a sense of joy in his heart, was nearer and dearer to God than the learned but joyless individual who spent his whole life in the study of Talmud. The essence of faith, he taught, lies in the emotions, not the intellect.

All Hasidic leaders referred to as *rebbes*, believed that vocal music is the best medium for approaching God. They felt that the power of melody was such that it could reach the heavens faster and be more acceptable to God than spoken prayer. The ecstasy of melody is the key with which Hasidism strived to unlock the gates of heaven. It is, so to speak, the "ladder to the throne of God."

Each major Hasidic dynasty had its own court, as the residence of the rebbe was called. It was the custom of Hasidim to spend major holidays at the rebbe's court, and devotees of various leaders would leave their homes and families, often traveling great distances, in order to spend a festival in the presence of the rebbe. Specific Sabbaths were also set aside for "get-togethers" of rebbe and followers. It was at these occasions that new melodies were introduced and old ones resung.

Most of the original Hasidic melodies were created by the leaders themselves, among them: Rabbi Shneur Zalman of Liadi (founder of *Chabad*), Rabbi Nachman of Bratslav, Rabbi Levi Yitzchok of Berditchev and the Rebbes of Modzitz. Where the rebbes did not posess musical creativity, their sons, or musically talented Hasidim, were appointed as "court composers." The new tunes were taught during Sabbath and festive gatherings, and, by the time the Hasid returned home, he was equipped to teach the new material to his family, friends and neighbors. Thus, without the advantage of yet-to-come recording devices, and musical transcriptions, these melodies became familiar household songs throughout eastern Europe.

In its very early stages Hasidic song was largely a graft of diversified elements of the surroundings, especially Moldavia and the Ukraine. It is known that almost every folk music contains within itself foreign elements. The contacts between various lands, the relationship between countries, the wars which occurred, all had a share in bringing about a musical hybridization. The interesting and surprising thing about Hasidic music is that it could take the foreign elements of the surrounding cultures and create a unique body of song with its own characteristics.

The majority of the early Hasidic songs were wordless. *Nigunim*, songs without words but full of religious ecstasy, were created on the premise that a song without words is much better than one with words. According to Rabbi Shneur Zalman, a melody with text, is limited in time, for, with the conclusion of the words, the melody, too, comes to an end. But a tune without words can be repeaed endlessly. To fill the need created by the absence of text, Hasidim invented a group of vocalized syllables which aided in the production of the song. The singer was at liberty to vocalize as he felt the mood of the music itself. Syllables such as *bim bom*, *dai dai*, *aha aha*, *yam bam*, etc. had no specific order or pattern. It was common practice for Hasidim to accept a specific group of vocalized syllables for their melodies. It is therefore possible for a trained listener to pinpoint the area of origin and the general authorship of a specific tune, on the basis of the syllables employed.

CHABAD *NIGUNIM*

About twelve years after the passing of the *Baal Shem Tov*, Lubavitch Hasidism, also known as ChaBaD, [an acronym formed from the initial letters of the words *Chochmo* (wisdom), *Binoh* (understanding) and *Da'as* (knowledge), became a powerful force within Hasidism. While *Chabad* drew from the fountainhead of the *Baal Shem Tov's* philosophy, it developed its own flavor and characteristics. Rabbi Shneur Zalman of Liadi, known as the *Alter Rebbe*, founder of the *Chabad* movement, deepened and broadened the philosophy of Hasidism. He also discovered new depths in Hasidic song. While the *Baal Shem Tov* revived song in Jewish life, the *Alter Rebbe* revealed the inner soul of Hasidic melody. His ten famous melodies became the archetype of all *Chabad* song. Several of these "holy" songs, including the *Alter Rebbe's Nigun*, are sung only at specific occasions.

The succeeding leaders of Lubavitch carried on the tradition of music established by Rabbi Shneur Zalman. The court of the *Mitler Rebbe*, Rabbi Dov Ber (son of the *Alter Rebbe* and second generation of *Chabad* leaders), had an established orchestra and choral group that inspired the Rebbe and his Hasidim at various gatherings. Also, in the time of the *Tsemach Tsedek*, Rabbi Menachem Mendel (grandson of the *Alter Rebbe* and son-in-law of the *Mitler Rebbe*), and in the time of his son, the *Rebbe Maharash* (Rabbi Samuel, fourth of the *Chabad* dynasty), hundreds of *nigunim* were composed.

Rabbi Yoseph Yitschok, sixth leader of *Chabad*, emphasized in his Hasidic dissertations the importance of *neginah*. After arriving on American shores in 1940, he transplanted many Lubavitcher activities to this country. The Rebbe also developed a plan to collect and perpetuate *Chabad nigunim*. In 1944, he founded the *Nichoach* Society whose purpose was to collect *Chabad nigunim* from various sources, determine their authentic versions, have the melodies notated, and preserve them in sheet music book form, and, eventually, in phonograph recordings. The first volume of *Sefer Hanigunim*, containing 175 melodies in music notation and historical background, was published in 1948. Rabbi Menachem Mendel Schneerson, the seventh generation of *Chabad* leaders, also strongly encouraged the work of *Nichoach*. Upon his initiative, a second volume of *Sefer Hanigunim* was issued in 1957. The Rebbe instructed that a series of recordings featuring select *nigunim* of *Chabad* be issued. The Rebbe pointed out that spreading Hasidic song was an integral part of *Chabad's* central mission, namely, the dissemination throughout the Jewish world of the Hasidic teaching and way of life as taught by the *Baal Shem Tov.*

MUSIC OF MODZITZ

Nowhere within Hasidism did music assume a greater role than in the dynasty of Modzitz. Music and Modzitz became synonymous. In his book, *Lahasidim Mizmor* (Jerusalem 1955), the eminent authority on the music of the Hasidim, M.S. Geshuri, compares the city of Modzitz, and its influence on the musical life of Eastern European Jewry, to Bayreuth and its affect on the devotees of Richard Wagner. The rabbinic dynasty in Modzitz was founded by Rabbi Yisroel Taub 1848-1920. In 1888, upon the death of his father, Rabbi Samuel Eliyahu of Zvolyn, Rabbi Yisroel assumed the leadership of Kuzmir-Zvolyn Hasidim. In 1891, he settled in Modzitz and resided there until the outbreak of World War I in 1914, when he fled to Warsaw. One of his most famous tunes, the *Heimloz Nigun* (the "Song of the Homeless"), was set to the text of Psalm 123, and became a Jewish classic. In it, the Rebbe gives musical expression to the feelings of a Jew torn from his home due to war.

Modzitz philosophy explains the emphasis on music and musical creativity. Rabbi Yisroel pointed to the word *habocher* which appears in two blessings, one preceding the *Barchu* prayer of the *Shacharit* service, and the other recited immediately before the reading of the *Haftorah*. In the first instance, the text reads *habocher b'shire zimro* (Blessed are You O Lord Our God who is pleased with songs and hymns), while the second blessing contains the words *habocher batorah* (Blessed are You O Lord our God who has chosen the Torah). These two *habocher*, Torah and melody, became the foundation of the Modzitz dynasty and its greatest contribution to Hasidic life.

The music of the Modzitz Rebbes became well known and beloved in almost every Polish city and hamlet in which Jews lived. Although small in comparison to such grand courts as Bobov, Ger, Lubavitch, Sanz, Belz, Vishnitz and others, Modzitz became a household word throughout the Jewish pale. The Modzitz Rebbes were the most prolific of all Hasidic composers. Rabbi Israel's output was approximately two hundred *nigunim*; Rabbi Saul's was approximately seven hundred (only about half survive); Rabbi Samuel Eliyahu's was approximately four hundred. Paying tribute to his father, Rabbi Israel, Rabbi Saul said, "Before my father, Hasidic music was mere folksong. He raised it to the level of art."

The wide popularity of Modzitz music is due primarily to a series of recordings first issued in the late 1950's and 60's.

"Hasidic Dancers by Tully Filmus

THE ALTER REBBES NIGUN

This *nigun* regarded as the "Holy of Holies" by Lubavitcher Hasidim is known both as the *Alter Rebbe's Nigun* and the *Rav's Nigun*. According to *Chabad*, Rabbi Shneur Zalman of Liadi, the Alter Rebbe, composed this *nigun* in 1799 during his imprisonment in Petersburg. The *nigun* is sung by Lubavitcher Hasidim each year on the 19th day of *Kislev*, which commemorates the anniversary of the freeing of the Rebbe from prison. It is also sung at weddings, Bar mitzvahs, circumcisions *Simchas Toroh* and on other joyous occasions throughout the year. Deep content is said to be hidden in the four sections of the *nigun*, and succeeding *Chabad* Rebbes brought forth many explanations to enable Hasidim to perceive their inner meanings. The *nigun* embodies the Rebbe's theory that melody should elevate the soul from the lowest to the highest spiritual regions.

The *Alter Rebbe's Nigun* begins slowly and sounds the first stage, the outpouring of the soul—*hishtapchus hanefesh*. Quickly the melody begins to pick up momentum and progresses to the second stage, the spiritual awakening— *hisor'rus* The third part aims to express the steps of *hithpaaluth*— the stage in which the individual is possessed by his thoughts, and *dvekus*—communion with God until it reaches the stage of ecstasy. The fourth part presents the stage of the "disembodied soul." According to later interpretation, however, the *Alter Rebbe's Nigun* gives tonal expression to the four realms of the universe. Beginning with *briah*—the creation of the lowest elements of minerals, it moves to the second higher realm, *y'tsira*—the creation of living beings. The tune progresses to the third realm, *asiya*—the creation of man, and reaches the goal in the fourth realm, *atsiluth*—emanation, the heavenly region.

Every *Chabad* tune aims to voice either all the stages of elevation, or only some phases of them. The last two stages are also called *Rikud* (dance).

Alter Rebbes Nigun

Siman Tov

Si-man tov u-ma-zl tov
Y'hé la-nu u-l'chol Yis-ra-él

סִימָן טוֹב וּמַזָּל טוֹב
יְהֵא לָנוּ וּלְכָל יִשְׂרָאֵל

May good fortune come to us and to all Israel.

This is the most popular *simcha* song which is appropriate
for any joyous Jewish occasion.

A Dudele

O Lord of the world, I will sing You a *"dudele"*. Where can you be found and where can You not be found? Wherever I go and wherever I stand You are there. You, only You, always You. Prosperity is from You, and suffering also comes from You. You are, You were, and You will always be. East, west, north and south are Yours. Heaven and earth are Yours. You take care of the high and the lowly. Wherever I turn, You are there.

רִבּוֹנוֹ שֶׁל עוֹלָם
כ׳וועל דיר א ״דודעלע זינגען״ דו....
אַיֵּה אֶמְצָאֶךָ וְאַיֵּה לֹא אֶמְצָאֶךָ
וואו קען מען דיך יא געפינען
אַן וואו קען מען דיך ניט געפינען. דו....
אז וואו איך גיה – דו. אן וואו איך שטיי – דו
רק דו, נאר דו, וידער דו, אבער דו דו....
איך עמיצען גוט – דו אן חלילה שלעכט – דו
מִזְרָח – דו, מַעֲרָב – דו, צָפוֹן – דו, דָּרוֹם – דו
שָׁמַיִם – דו אָרֶץ – דו, מַעֲלָה – דו, מַטָּה – דו
וואו איך קער מיך, וואו איך וועגד מיך – דו.

This song, in the liturgical-recitative style perfected by Rabbi Levi Yitschok of Berditchev (1740-1810), has become a favorite of singers throughout the world. The text is in Yiddish, and the title of the song is a play on two words: *"du"* ("you,") in this case God, and the primitive shepherd's instrument, the *dudelsack* (bagpipe).

Eli Ata

Lento religioso

Eli Ata v'-o-de-ka E-lo-hai a-ro-m'-me-ka

אֵלִי אַתָּה וְאוֹדֶךָ אֱלֹהַי אֲרוֹמְמֶךָ

You are my God and I will give thanks to You.
You are my God and I will exult You.

Eli Ata is one of the ten *nigunim* composed by the Alter Rebbe, founder of Lubavitch Hasidism. For many generations it was the custom of the Lubavitcher Rebbes to sing this *nigun* at the close of the Passover *Seder* while pouring wine from Elijah's cup back into the decanter. The melody is set to a text from the *Hallel* Service recited on the Festivals. For Lubavitcher Hasidim *Eli Ato* is a heartfelt declaration of thankfulness, spiritual satisfaction, and belief in the future redemption through the coming of the Messiah.

A Din Toire Mit Got

Recitativo religioso

Gu_ten mor_gen dir ri_bo_no shel o_lom, ich Lê_vi yitz_chok ben soroh mibar_dit_shev,

ch'bin ge_ku_men tzu dir mit a din to_roh fun dein folk yis_ro_êl, vos host du tzu dein

folk yis_ro_êl, vos host du zich on_ge_setzt on dein folk yis_ro_êl, az vu nor a_zach iz

e_mor el be_nê yis_ro_êl, az vu nor a_zach iz tzav el be_nê yis_ro_êl, az vu nor a_

zach iz da_bêr el be_nê yis_ro_êl, ta_te_niu zi_ser in himmel, ka_moh u_mos yêsh be_o_lom?

par_sa_yim, bav_la_yim a_do_ma_yim. die Russ_lander vos zo_gen? az zei_er Kai_ser iz Kai_ser.
die Deitschlander vos zo_gen? az zei_er mal_chus is mal_chus,

die Englander vos zogen az zei_er mal_chus iz mê_lech, un ich Lê_vi yitz_chok ben so_

roh mi_bar_dit_shev zog: yis_ga_dal ve_yiska_dach shemê ra_boh! un ich Lê_vi yitz_chok ben

so_roh mi_bar_dit_shev zog: lô o_zuz mim_kô_mi, ich vel mich fun ort nicht rih_ren, un a sôf

zol dos nehmen, un an ek zol dos neh_men, yis_ga_dal ve_yis_ka_desh she_mê ra_boh.

134

'"Good morning, Master of the universe
I, Levi Yitschok of Berditchev
Have come to hold judgment with You
Concerning Your people Israel
What have You against Israel?
Why have you imposed Yourself
Upon Your people Israel?
Everywhere You say:
Command the children of Israel.
Everywhere-Speak to the children of Israel.
Father of mercy
How many nations are there in the world?
Persians, Babylonians, Romans
The Russians— what do they say?
That their emperor is ruler
The Germans—what do they say?
That their Kaiser is King
The English—what do they say?
That their king is ruler
But I Levi-Yitzchok of Berditchev, say
Magnified and sanctified be the Great Name
And I Levi-Yitzchok of Berditchev say:
I will not move from this place, from this very spot
Until there will be an end,
Until there will be an end to this exile
Magnified and sanctified be the Great Name"

This song is also known as *The Kaddish of Reb Levi Yitzchok*. The author, Rabbi Levi Yitschok of Berditchev, knew that Yiddish was the language understood by the common masses. Although Hebrew was part of the daily services, the ordinary Jew found great difficulty in understanding it fully.

Ki Onu Amecho

Ki o-nu a-me-cho v'-ato E-lo-ké-nu o-nu vo-ne-cho

V'a-to o-vi-nu o-nu k'-ho-le-cho v'-a-to chel-ké-nu

O-nu na-cha-lo-se-cho v'-a-to go-ro-lé-nu

כִּי אָנוּ עַמֶּךְ וְאַתָּה אֱלוֹקֵינוּ אָנוּ בָנֶיךָ
וְאַתָּה אָבִינוּ אָנוּ קְהָלֶךָ וְאַתָּה חֶלְקֵנוּ
אָנוּ נַחֲלָתֶךָ וְאַתָּה גוֹרָלֵנוּ

For we are Your people and You are our God. We are your children and
You our Father. We are Your servants and You our Master. We are Your
Congregation and You are our Portion.

The Lubavitcher Rebbe taught this melody after *Hakofos* in 1964. He had heard it from an old hasid who sang the melody to the words *Ki Onu Amecho* during the Yom Kippur prayers. Upon conclusion of the fast, he broke out in a fervent dance, singing the same melody and repeating the words again and again

Hop Cossack

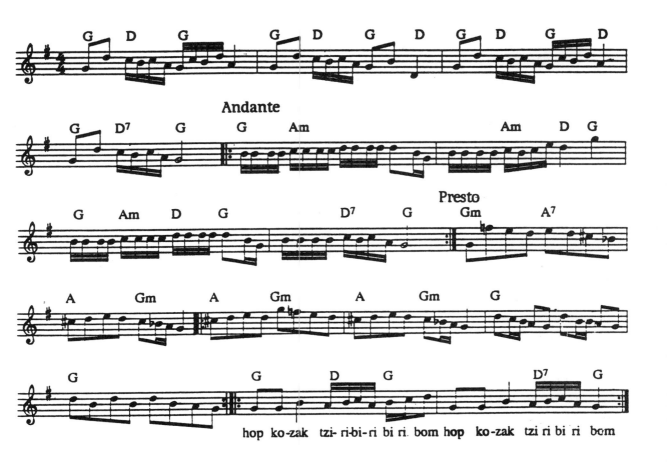

hop ko-zak tzi- ri-bi-ri bi ri. bom hop ko-zak tzi ri bi ri bom

The *pritzim* (nobles) ruling the villages in old Russia and Ukraine during the *Shpoler Zayde's* (a disciple of the *Baal Shem Tov*) time, used to make sport with their Jewish subjects by dressing them in bearskins and forcing them to dance with a Cossack. If the Jew failed to keep step with the tune, he would be whiplashed. Once a Jew was imprisoned for failing to pay his rent on time. When he was forced to dance in a bearskin the *Shpoler Zayde* took his place. Because the *Shpoler Zayde's* dancing was superior, he gained an upper hand over the Cossack. *Hop Cossack* gives musical expression to this incident by opening slowly, gradually working to a climax and the victorious cry "hop Cossack." For Hasidim of Lubavitch this song is meant to spur fervent and joyous worship of God. It is sung on *Simchas Torah* and other joyous occasions.

YIDDISH FOLK SONG

According to a number of scholars, the The Yiddish language originated in the Rhine Basin around 1000 C.E. Like Hebrew and Aramaic, this is a language with a structure of its own. As early as the 17th century, it had already developed a unique set of dialects quite different from those of German. It was spoken by Jewish communities in Southern, Central, and Northern Germany, Bohemia, Poland, Lithuania, Northern Italy, Ukraine, and Holland, and reached its widest usage in the 18th century. Then it declined in Italy and Germany but expanded anew in the Western Hemisphere, Palestine, Australia, and South Africa. Before World War II, some eleven million Jews spoke Yiddish.

The Yiddish folksong of Eastern Europe is the creation of the Jewish masses living in the Slavic countries, especially in Poland, Ukraine, Lithuania and Southern Russia, as well as those in Hungary and Rumania. Its creation covers the period from the end of the 16th century to modern times. Although Yiddish folk song began to vanish from Western and Central Europe during the early part of the 19th century, Jewish secular folk song, recast in modern Yiddish vernacular, burst into full bloom in the Slavic lands. Many new categories of secular song now welled from the depths of the people, including cradle songs, ballads and dance songs, drinking and humorous songs, work and children's songs, soldier and topical songs, nonsense and satirical songs, ethical and historical songs, as well as those for weddings and holidays. In the Slavic countries, the Jew instinctively turned toward his neighbor's Oriental folk music that was melodically close to his own song. Before Idelsohn's *Hebrew-Oriental Thesaurus* was published, relatively few tunes had been preserved in written form.

Although the majority of Yiddish songs are secular, there are also a number of religious songs. The texts of the songs are partly in Hebrew and partly in Yiddish. Some songs are bilingual—Hebrew-Yiddish, Yiddish-Ukrainian, Yiddish Russian etc. Some are comprised of three languages, Hebrew-Yiddish-Slavic etc. Among the texts are those which describe the miseries of the Jewish masses in Eastern Europe, especially under the Czarist regimes; songs that relate to the terrible economic conditions and those songs that portray the battle between old and new beliefs and customs. The texts often bewail the fate of the Jewish woman who carried heavy burdens and was usually the supporter of the family. In addition, there are texts which depict the revolutionary movement in Russia and Jewish participation in that movement. In these songs, the whole scale of life of the Jewish folk can be seen; all ranks of the Jewish people speak, from the highest to the lowest, from the rabbi and Talmudic scholar to the thief, and from the mother to the prostitute. The Yiddish folk song of the Eastern Europe mirrors Jewish life in the 19th and the 20th centuries until the Second World War.

Folk song for the most part, just grows. Composers of the tunes are rarely identified or remembered. In the Yiddish folk song, occasionally the composer's name lives on with a tune. For example, Mark Warshawsky, Abraham Goldfaden and Mordechai Gebirtig are names that co-relate with their creations. Popular songs in folk style, composed by well-known original folk entertainers—*badchonim*—have become part of the Jewish musical heritage. These songs lived in the memory of the people. The *badchan* par excellence was Elyakum Zunser (Vilna 1838-New York 1913), the most prominent Jewish bard of Eastern Europe. According to his own statement, he composed 600 songs with texts and music only a few of which were published during his lifetime. Many of his songs became exceedingly popular. He performed his art at many Jewish weddings. None of the above mentioned folksingers had any formal music training, but their creations are in the typical style of Jewish folk song and show all of the inherent characteristics.

In the 20th century Yiddish folksongs were kept alive both on stage and in numerous recordings. The following are among the recognized American Yiddish singers: Theodore Bikel, The Barry Sisters, Jan Peerce, Richard Tucker, Mordecai Hershman, Sidor Belarsky, Miriam Kressyn, Seymour Rechtseit, and Leibele Waldman. A number of well-known singers including, Nekhama Liphshutz, Isa Kramer, Bente Kahn, Dudu Fisher, Misha Alexandrovitch, and others performed and recorded Yiddish in Europe and Israel.

Sheet music folios—early 20th century

Yidishe Ma-me

Yiddishe Mame is the most popular song dedicated to the Jewish mother. The song has been a mainstay in the repertoire of singers of Yiddish since 1925.

Ich vil bai aich a ka-she fré-gen	איך וויל ביי אייך א קאשיא פרעגן
Zogt mir ver es ken	זאגט מיר ווער עס קען
Mit vel-che ta-ye-re far-me-gens	מיט וועלכע טאיערע פערמעגנס
Bentsht Got a-le-men	בענטשט גאט אלעמען
Men koift es nit far ké-ne gelt	מען קויפט עס ניט פאר קיינע געלט
Dos git men nor um-zist	דאס גיט מען נאר אומזיסט
Un doch az men far-lirt dos	און דאך אז מען פארלירט דאס
Vi fil tre-ren men far-gist	ווי פיהל טרערן מען פארגיסט
A tsvé-te git men ké-nem nit	א צווייטע גיט מען קיינעם ניט
Es helft nit kain ge-vén	עס העלפט ניט קיין געוויין
Oi ver es hot far-loi-ren	אוי ווער עס האט פארלוירן
Der vés shoin vos ich mén	דער ווייס שוין וואס איך מיין
A yi-di-she ma-me	א אידישע מאמע
Es gibt nit be-ser in der velt	עס גיבט ניט בעסער אין דער וועלט
A yi-di-she ma-me	א אידישע מאמע
Oi vé vi bi-ter ven zi félt	אוי ווי ווי ביטער ווען זי פעהלט
Vi shén un lich-tig iz in hoiz	ווי שיין אונד ליכטיג איז אין הויז
Ven di ma-me 'z do	ווען די מאמעיז דא
Vi troi-rig fin-ster vert	ווי טרויריג פינסטער ווערט
Ven Got nemt ir oif o-lom ha-bo	ווען גאט נעמט איהר אויף עוֹלָם הַבָּא
In vas-er un fa-yer	אין וואסער אונד פייער
Volt zi ge-lof-en far ir kind	וואלט זי געלאפן פאר איהר קינד
Nit halt-en ir ta-yer	ניט האלטן איהר טייער
Dos iz ge-vis di gres-te zind	דאס איז געוויס די גרעסטע זינד
Oi vi glik-lich und raich	אוי ווי גליקליך אונד רייך
Iz der mentsh vos hot	איז דער מענטש וואס האט
A za shé-ne ma-to-ne ge-shenkt fun Got	א זא שיינע מתנה געשענקט פון גאט
Nor ain alt-itsh-ke Yi-di-she ma-me	נאר איין אלטיטשקע אידישע מאמע
Ma-me main	מאמע מיין

Singable English Setting

My Yidishe ma-me I need her more than ever now
My Yidishe ma-me I'd like to kiss her wrinkled brow
I long to hold her hand once more as in days gone by
And ask her to forgive me for things I did that made her cry
How few were her pleasures, she never cared for fashion styles
Her jewels and her treasures she found in her baby's smiles
O I know that I owe what I am today
To that dear little lady who's young yet gray
To that wonderful Yidishe ma-me
Ma-me mine.

Donna Donna

Text: A. Zeitlin
Music: Sholom Secunda
English Lyrics: Sheldon Secunda

Originally titled *Dana, Dana, Dana*, the song was written by Sholom Secunda and published in 1943. It became one of the most widely sung Jewish songs and was performed in Yiddish, Hebrew and English translation by Theodore Bikel, Joan Baez and others. Because of the lyrics, *Calves are easily bound and slaughtered, never knowing the reason why*, the song was mistakenly attributed to the Holocaust. Translations have also appeared in German and Korean.

144

On a wagon bound for market
There's a calf with a mournful eye
High above him there's a swallow
Winging swiftly through the sky
Refrain
How the winds are laughing
They laugh with all their might
Laugh and laugh the whole day through
And half a summer's night
Donna donna donna ....

"Stop complaining," said the farmer
"Who told you a calf to be
Why don't you have wings to fly with
Like the swallow so proud and free?" *Refrain*

Calves are easily bound and slaughtered
Never knowing the reason why
But whoever treasures freedom
Like the swallow has learned to fly   *Refrain*

Oi-fen furl ligt dos kel-bel
Ligt ge-bun-den mit a shtrik
Hoich in him-el flit dos shvel-bel
Frét zich drét zich hin un krik
Refrain
Lacht der vint in korn
Lacht un lacht un lacht
Lacht er op a tog a gan-tsen
Mit a hal-ber nacht
Dona dona dona........

Shrait dos kel-bel zogt der poi-er
Ver zhe hést dich zain a kalb
Volst ge-kert tsu zain a foi-gel
Volst ge-kert tsu zain a shvalb   *Refrain*

Kel-ber tut men bin-den
Un men shlept zé un men shecht
Ver s'hot fli-gel flit a-roif-tsu
Iz bai ké-nem nit kain knecht   *Refrain*

אופן פורל ליגט דאס קעלבל
ליגט געבונדן מיט א שטריק
הויך אין הימל פליט דאס שוועלבל
פרייט זיך דרייט זיך הין און קריק
רעפריין
לאכט דער וינט אין קארן
לאכט און לאכט און לאכט
לאכט ער אפ א טאג א גאנצן
מיט א האלבער נאכט
דאנא, דאנא, דאנא..........

שרייט דאס קעלבל זאגט דער פויער
ווער זשע הייסט דיך זיין א קאלב?
וואלסט געקערט צו זיין א פויגל
וואלסט געקערט צו זיין א שוואלב רעפריין

קעלבער טוט מען בינדן
און מען שלעפט זיי און מען שעכט
ווער ס'האט פליגל פליט ארויפצו
איז ביי קיינעם ניט קיין קנעכט רעפריין

145

Belz

Moderately

Belz main shté-te-le Belz	בעלז-מיין שטעטעלע בעלז
Main hé-me-le vu ich hob	מיין היימעלע וװ איך האב
Mai-ne kinder-she yorn far-bracht	מײנע קינדערשע יארן פארבראכט
Zait ir a mol geven in Belz,	זײט איר א מאל געװען אין
Main shté-tele Belz	בעלז-מיין שטעטעלע בעלז
In o-re-men shti-be-le	אין ארעמען שטיבעלע
Mit ale kin-der-lech dort ge-lacht	מיט אלע קינדערלעך דארט געלאכט
Yé-dn Sha-bos fleg ich loi-fn	יעדן שבת פלעג איך לויפן
Dort mit der tchi-na glaich	דארט מיט דער תְחִינָה גלײך
Tsu zit-sn un-ter dem gri-nem bé-me-le	צו זיצן אונטער דעם גרינעם ביימעלע
Lé-nen bai dem taich	לײענען ביי דעם טײך
Belz main shté-te-le Belz	בעלז-מיין שטעטעלע בעלז
Main hé-me-le vu ch'-hob ge-hat	מיין היימעלע וװ איך האב געהאט
Di shé-ne cha-lo-mes a sach	די שײנע חלומות א סך

Belz, my little town, the home where I spent my childhood years. Every Sabbath I would run down to read by the river. Belz, my little town where I had so many wonderful dreams.

Belz one of the most popular Yiddish theater songs of the 20th century was written for the play *Song of the Ghetto* by the noted Yiddish Theater composer Alexander Olshanetsky. The song is an expression of longing for the East European *shtetl*.

Shén Vi Di L'vone

Shén vi di l'-vo-ne	שיין ווי די לבנה
Lech-tig vi di shte-ren	לעכטיג ווי די שטערן
Fun hi-ml a ma-to-ne	פון הימל א מתנה
Bis-tu mir tsu-ge-shikt	ביסטו מיר צוגעשיקט
Main glik hob ich ge-vun-en	מיין גליק האב איך געוואונען
Ven ich hob dich ge-fun-en	ווען איך האב דיך געפונען
Di shainst vi toi-zent zun-en	די שיינסט ווי טויזנט זונען
Du host main hartz ba-glikt	דו האסט מיין הארץ באגליקט
Dai-ne tsén-da-lach vai-se pe-re-lach	דיינע ציינדאלעך ווייסע פערלעך
Mit dai-ne shé-ne oi-gen	מיט דיינע שיינע אויגן
Dai-ne chén-de-lech dai-ne her-a-lech	דיינע חנדעלעך דיינע הערלעך
Host mich tsu-ge-tsoi-gen	האסט מיך צוגעצויגן
Shén vi di l'-vo-ne	שיין ווי די לבנה
Lech-tig vi di shte-rn	לעכטיג ווי די שטערן
Fun hi-ml a ma-to-ne	פון הימל א מתנה
Bis-tu mir tsu-ge-shikt	ביסטו מיר צוגעשיקט

Pretty as the moon, bright as the stars, you are a heaven-sent gift to me.

Menashe Skulnik the famed comedic Yiddish actor used to say that this song was especially written for him. He stopped performing *Shén Vi Di L'vone* when it became a big hit and was sung by many other Yiddish singers.

Rumania Rumania

di - gi di - gi dam; Hai di - gi di - gi dam di - gi di - gi di - gi dam

Hai di - gi di - gi di - gi di - gi di - gi dam. Oy vey g'vald, ich ver m' - shu - ge,

ch'lib nor brin - ze ma - me - li - ge, ch'tants un fré zich biz der stel - ye,

ven ich es a pat - lo - zhe - le Dzing - ma tai ti - dl di dam Dzing - ma, tai

ti - dl di dam Dzing - ma, tai ti - dl di dam Dzing - ma tai ti dl di dam

Ai s'iz a m' - cha - ye be - ser ken nit zain ai a

far - ge - ni - gn iz nor Ru - mé - nish vain A_____

Y' - kum pur - kon min sh' - ma - yo shté un kusht di kech - ne Cha - ya on - ge - ton in

al - te shkra - bes macht a ku - gl l'ko - ved Sha - bos Zets! tai ti - dl di dam

151

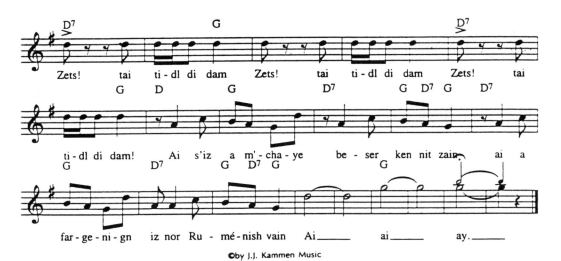

©by J.J. Kammen Music

Ech Rumania Rumania........	עך רומעניע רומעניע.............
Ge-ven a mol a land a zi-se a shé-ne	געווען א מאל א לאנד א זיסע א שיינע
Ech Rumania Rumania........	עך רומעניע רומעניע.............
Ge-ven a mol a land a zi-se a fai-ne	געווען א מאל א לאנד א זיסע א פיינע
Dort tsu voi-nen iz a far-ge-ni-gen	דארט צו וואוינען איז א פארגעניגען
Vos dos hartz glust dir	וואס דאס הארץ גלוסט דיר
Dos ken-stu kri-gen	דאס קענסטו קריגען
A ma-me-li-ge-le a pas-tra-me-le	א מאמעליגעלע א פאסטראמעלע
A kar-na-tsa-le un a glé-ze-le vain	א קארנאצעלע און א גלעזעלע וויין
In Rumania iz doch git	אין רומעניע איז דאך גיט
Fun kain dai-ges vest men nit	פון קיין דאגעס ווייסט מען ניט
Vain trinkt men iber-al	וויין טרינקט מען איבעראל
Me far-baist mit kash-ta-val	מע פארבייסט מיט קאשטאוואל
Hai digidigidigidam digidigidigidam....	הי דינידיניאם דינידינידאם........
Oi ge-vald ich ver m'-shu-ga	אוי געוואלד איך ווער משוגע
'Ch lib nor brin-ze ma-me-li-ge	כליב נאר ברינזע מאמעליגע
'Ch tantz un fré zich biz der stel-ye	כטאנץ און פריי זיך ביז דער סטעליע
Ven ich es a pat-la-ze-le	ווען איך עס א פאטלאזשעלע
Dzing ma tai ti-di-di dam....	דזינג-מא טיי טידידי דאם.........
Ai 's -iz a m'-cha-ye be-ser ken nit zain	אי סאיז א מחיה בעסער קען ניט זיין
Ai a far-ge-ni-gen iz nor Ru-mé-nish vain	אי א פארגעניגען איז נאר רומעניש וויין
Y-'kum pur-kon min sh'-ma-yo	יקום פורקן מין שמיא
Shtet un kusht di kech-ne cha-ye	שטייט און קושט די קעכנע חיה
On-ge-ton in al-te shkra-bes	אנגעטאן אין אלטע שקראבעס
Macht a ku-gel l'ko-ved Sha-bos	מאכט א קוגעל לכבוד שבת
Tai tidldidam zets taitidldidam	טי טידלדידאם זעטס טידלדידאם.........
Ai 's iz a m'-cha-ye be-ser ken nit zain	אי סאיז א מחיה בעסער קען ניט זיין
Ai a far-ge-ni-gen iz nor Ru-mé-nish vain	אי א פארגעניגען איז נאר רומעניש וויין

Ah! Rumania Rumania. It was once a beautiful country. To live there
was a pleasure. Pastrami, mamalige and above all wonderful wine.

Rumania, Rumania became one of the standards of the Yiddish Theater and has
remained popular. Aaron Lebedeff one of the luminaries of the Yiddish stage
composed it over a period of years. Lebedeff added and deleted material in
response to the reactions of his audiences. Finally set by Sholom Secunda the
famed conductor and composer of Yiddish Theater on Second Avenue in New
York City, it was recorded by Lebedeff and numerous other singers.

Der Rebe Elimelech

Az der Re-be E-li-me-lech iz ge - vo-ren zé-er fré-lach iz ge- vo-ren zé-er fré-lach E-li - me-lech hot er ois-ge-ton di tfi-len un hot on-ge-ton di bri-len un hot ge - shikt noch di fi - dler di tzvé un az di fi - del - di - ke fid - ler ho - bn fid - el - dik ge - fid - elt ho - bn fid - el dik ge - fid elt ho - bn zé un az di fid el - di - ke fid - ler ho - bn fid - el - dik ge - fid elt ho - bn fid el - dik ge - fid - elt ho - bn zé

Az der Re-be E-li-me-lech	אז דער רבי אלימלך
Iz ge-vorn zé-er fré-lach,	איז געוואָרן זייער פריילעך
Is ge-vorn zé-er fré-lech Eli-me-lech	איז געוואָרן זייער פריילעך אלימלך
Hot er ois-ge-ton di t'-filn	האָט ער אויסגעטאָן די תפילין
Un hot on-ge-ton di bri-ln	און האָט אנגעטאָן די ברילן
Un ge-shikt noch di fid-lers di tsvé	און געשיקט נאָך די פידלערס די צוויי
Un di fidl-di-ke fid-lers	און די פידלדיקע פידלערס
Hobn fidl-dik ge-fidlt	האָבן פידלדיק געפידלט
Hobn fidl-dik ge-fidlt hobn zé	האָבן פידלדיק געפידלט האָבן זיי

When Rabbi Elimelech became merry he removed his phylacteries, put on his
glasses and summoned his two fiddlers. The fiddlers truly fiddled.

Composed by Moshe Nadir (1885-1943), *Der Rebbe Elimelech*, a Yiddish version of
the English song *Old King Cole*, is one of the most popular Yiddish songs of all time.

Papirosn

A kal - te - nacht a né - bl - di - ke fins - ter u - me - tum

Shtét a yin - ge - le far - troi - ert Un kukt zich a - rum fun ré - gn shitst im nor a vant a

ko - shi - kl trogt er in hant un zai - ne oi - gn bé - tn yé - dn shtum. Ich

hob shoin nit kain ko - ach mer a - rum - tsu - gén in gas hun - ge - rik un op - ge - ri - sn

fun dem re - gn nas ich shlep a - rum zich fun ba - gi - nen ké - ner git nit tsu far - di - nen

A - le la - chn ma - chn fun mir shpas.____ Ku - pit - ye koift zhe koift__ pa - pi -

ro - sn tru - ke - ne fun ré - gn nit far - go - sn

Koift zhe bi - lik b' - n' - mo - nes Koift un hot oif mir rach - mo - nes ra - te - vet fun hun - ger mich a -

tsind____ ku - pit - ye koift zhe shvé - be - lech an - ti - kn der

mit vet ir a yo - so - ml der - kvi - kn um - zist main shrai - en un main loi - fn

ké - ner vil bai mir nit koi - fn oys - gén vel ich mu - zn vi a hunt.

©by J.J. Kammen Music

A kal-te nacht a ne-bel-di-ge	א קאלטע נאכט א נעבעלדיגע
Fins-ter u-me-tum	פינסטער אומעטום
Shtét a yin-ge-le frar-troi-ert	שטייט א אינגעלע פארטרוויערט
Un kukt zich a-rum	און קוקט זיך ארום
Fun ré-gn shtitst im nor a vant	פון רעגן שיצט אים נאר א וואנט
A ko-shi-kl halt er in hant	א קאשיקל האלט ער אין האנט
Un zai-ne oi-gen be-tn yé-dn shtum	און זיינע אויגן בעטן יעדן שטום
Ich hob shoin nisht kain ko-ach mer	איך האב שוין ניט קיין כח מעהר
A-rum-tsu-gén in gas	ארומצוגיין אין גאס
Hun-ge-rik un op-ge-ri-sn	הונגעריק און אפגעריסן
Fun dem re-gn nas	פון דעם רעגן נאס
Ich shlep a-rum zich fun ba-ni-gen	איך שלעפ ארום זיך פון באניגען
Ké-ner git nit tsu far-di-nen	קיינער גיט ניט צו פארדינען
A-le la-chn ma-chn fun mir shpas	אלע לאכן מאכן פון מיר שפאס
Ku-pit-ye koift- zhe koift-zhe pa-pi-ro-sn	קופיטיע קויפט זשע קויפט זשע פאפיראסן
Tru-ke-ne fun re-gn nit far-go-sn	טרוקענע פון רעגן ניט פארגאסן
Koift- zhe bil-ik b'-ne-mo-nes	קויפט זשע ביליק בנאמנות
Koift un hot oif mir rach-mo-nes	קויפט און האט אויף מיר רחמנות
Ra-te-vet fun hun-ger mich a-tsind	ראטעוועט פון הונגער מיך אצינד
Ku-pit-ye koift- zhe shvé-ba-lach an-ti-kn	קופיטיע קויפט זשע שוועבאלאך אנטיקן
Der mit vet ir a yo-simi der-kvi kn	דער. מיט וועט איר א יתוסיל דערקוויקן
Um-zist main shrai-en un main loi-fn	אומזיסט מיין שרייען און מיין לויפן
Ké-ner vil bai mir nit koi-fn	קיינער וויל ביי מיר ניט קויפן
Ois-gén vel ich mu-zn vi a hunt	אויסגיין וועל איך מוזן ווי א הונט

On a cold, misty night a hungry little boy tries to sell cigarettes. "Buy from me," he cries "save me from starvation."

Herman Yablokoff, who as a child peddled cigarettes, introduced *Papirosn* on radio station WEVD in New York City prior to World War II. The song became an instant hit and thousands of sheet music folios were printed. With altered lyrics, *Papirosn* was also sung in the ghettos during the Holocaust.

Bai Mir Bistu Shén

Bai Mir Bistu Shén, is the most financially successful Yiddish song of all time. During the early days of his musical career, Sholom Secunda, the composer, sold the copyright for an insignificant sum. The song was recorded on November 24, 1937, by Patti, Maxine, and Laverne Andrew (The Andrew Sisters). In 1938, and for almost a decade to follow, it was the most popular Yiddish song in the United States.

Two differing stories are told about the origin of the recorded version of *Bai Mir Bistu Shén*. One relates that an agent, Lou Levy, brought the song to the Andrew sisters thinking that an all-Yiddish song sung by three Gentile girls could become a hit in New York City. Supposedly, they cut the demo in Yiddish, but the president of Decca Records insisted that English words would have to be used.

Another version is found in *I Should Care*, the autobiography of Sammy Cahn, the lyricist of the English version. Cahn says that he heard two black performers singing the song in Yiddish at the Appollo Theater in Harlem. Although the audience did not understand a single word, they seemed to enjoy the song. Cahn was impressed, so he bought the sheet music. He aroused the interest of the Andrew Sisters and they tried to convince Jack Kapp, the head of Decca Records, to let them record it. He agreed but only if Cahn would translate the words into English. The recorded version earned three million dollars for Decca. Towards the end of his life, the copyright reverted to Secunda, and he received royalties until his death.

156

un fin zé a le ois_____ ge-kli-bin hob ich nor dich_____

bai mir bis-tu shén   Bai mir hos-tu chén   bist

é-ne bai mir oif der velt._____   bai   velt._____

Ven du zolst zain shvarts vi a tu-ter	ווען דו זאלסט זיין שווארץ ווי א טאטער

Ven du zolst zain shvarts vi a tu-ter
Ven du host oi-gen vi a ku-ter
Un ven du hinkst tsu-bis-lach
Host hil-tser-ne fis-lach
Zog ich dos art mich nit
Un ven du host a nar-ish-en shmé-chel
Un ven du host Vai-zo-so's sé-chel
Ven du bist vild vi a In-di-a-ner
Bist a-fi-lu a Ga-lits-ya-ner
Zog ich dos art mich nit
Zog mir vi er-klers-tu dos?
'Ch-vel dir zog-en shoin far-vos
Vail bai mir bis-tu shén
Bai mir hos-tu chén
Bai mir bis-tu
E-ner oif der velt
Bai mir bis-tu git
Bai mir hos-tu "it"
Bai mir bis-tu ta-yer-er fun gelt
Fil shé-ne méd-lach hob-en
Shoin ge-volt nem-en mich
Un fun zé a-le ois-ge-klib-en
Hob ich nor dich
Vail bai mir bis-tu shén
Bai mir hos-tu chén
Bai mir bis-tu
E-ner oif der velt

ווען דו זאלסט זיין שווארץ ווי א טאטער
ווען די האסט אויגען ווי א קאטער
און ווען דו הינקסט צוביסלאך
האסט הילצערנע פיסלאך
זאג איך דאס ארט מיך ניט
און ווען דו האסט א נארישען שמייכעל
און ווען דו האסט וזתהיס שֵׂכֶל
ווען דו ביסט ווילד ווי א אינדיאנער
ביזט אפילו א גאליציאנער
זאג איך דאס ארט מיך ניט
זאג מיר ווי ערקלערהסטו דאס?
כ'וועל דיר זאגען שוין פארוואס
וויל ביי מיר ביסטו שעהן
ביי מיר האָסטו חֵן
ביי מיר ביסטו
איינער אויף דער וועלט
ביי מיר ביסטו גיט
ביי מיר האסטו "איט"
ביי מיר ביסטו טייערער פון געלט
פיל שעהנע מיידלאך האבען
שוין געוואלט נעמען מיך
און פון זיי אלע אויסגעקליבען
האב איך נאר דיך
ביי מיר ביסטו שעהן
ביי מיר האָסטו חֵן
ביי מיר ביסטו
איינער אויף דער וועלט

To me you are the most beautiful of all the young ladies. Many girls have been interested in me but from all of them I have chosen you.

157

Oifn Pripitchik

Cover of Mark Warshawsky's *Yudishe Folkslieder*, 1900

A rebbe (teacher) sits near the fireplace teaching his young students the mechanics of reading Hebrew. Originally titled, *Der Aleph Beyz* (The Alphabet), *Oyfn Pripitchik* was written by Mark Warshawsky (1840-1907). Its popularity has been so widespread that it is commonly thought to be a folksong. *Oyfn Pripitchik* served as a musical theme in a movie based on the life of Gershwin. Singable translations in English, as well as other languages, are quite common. During the Holocaust, a parody version circulated through the ghetto. The opening lyrics were: *At the ghetto wall a fire burns, the surveillance is keen.*

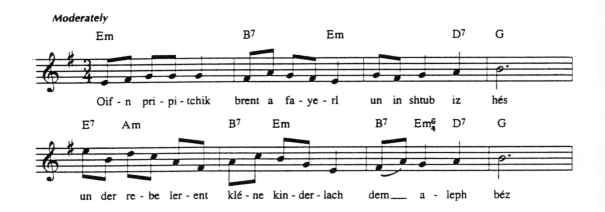

Oifn pri-pi-chik brent a fa-ye-rl	אויפן פריפעטשיק ברענט א פייערל	
Un in shtub iz hés	און אין שטוב איז הייס	
Un der re-be ler-ent klé-ne kin-der-lach	און דער רבי לערנט קלײנע קינדערלעך	
Dem a-leph béz	דעם אלף-בית	
Zét zhe kin-der-lach ge-denkt zhe ta-ye-re	זעט זשע קינדערלעך געדענקט זשע טײערע	
Vos ir ler-ent do	וואָס איר לערנט דא	
Zogt zhe noch a mol un ta-ke noch a mol	זאָגט זשע נאך א מאל און טאקע נאך א מאל	
Ko-mets a a-leph o	קמָץ-אַלָף אָ	

Lernt kin-der mit grois ché-shek	לערענט קינדער מיט גרויס חשק
A-zoi zog ich aich on	אזוי זאג איך אײך אן
Ver s'vet gi-cher fun aich ken-en iv-re	ווער ס׳וועט גיכער פון אײך קענען עברי
Der ba-kumt a fon *Refrain*	דער באקומט א פאן

Az ir vet kinder elter vern	אז איר וועט קינדער עלטער ווערן
Vet ir a-lén far-shtén	וועט איר אליין פארשטיין
Vi fil in di oi-syes li-gn trern	וויפל אין די אותיות ליגן טרערן
Un vi fil ge-vén *Refrain*	און ווי פיל געוויין

Az ir vet kin-der dem go-les shle-pn	אז איר וועט קינדער דעם גלות שלעפן
Ois-ge-mut-shet zain	אויסגעמוטשעט זיין
Zolt ir fun di oi-syes ko-ach shepn	זאלט איר פון די אותיות כח שיפן
Kukt in zé a-rain	קוקט אין זיי אריין

A flame burns in the fireplace and the room is warm. The teacher drills the children in the *alef-béz*. When you grow older you will understand that this alphabet contains the tears of our people. When you grow weary you will find comfort in this alphabet

159

Tumbalalaika

Moderately

The authorship of this popular song is unknown. Published for the first time in the United States (1940), *Tumbalalaika* appeared in numerous recordings including a version by the famed Barry Sisters. Although a number of varying texts have appeared, the lyrics in the form of a riddle, are the most popular.

Shtét a bo-cher un er tracht

שטייט א בחור און ער טראכט

Tracht un tracht a gan-tse nacht

טראכט און טראכט א גאנצע נאכט

Vé-men tsu ne-men un nisht far-she-men

וועמען צו נעמען און נישט פארשעמען

Ve-men tsu ne-men un nisht far-she-men

וועמען צו נעמען און נישט פארשעמען

Tum-bala tum-bala tum-balalaika

טום-באלא טום-באלא טום-באלאלייקע

Tum-bala tum-bala tum-balalaika

טום-באלא טום-באלא טום-באלאלייקע

Tum-balalaika shpil balalaika

טום-באלאלייקע שפיל באלאלייקע

Shpil balalaika fré-lech zol zain!

שפיל באלאלייקע פריילעך זאל זיין

Mé-dl mé-dl ch'vil bai dir fré-gn

מיידל, מיידל כ׳וויל ביי דיר פרעגן

Vos ken vak-sn vak-sn on ré-gn?

וואס קען וואקסן, וואקסן אן רעגן

Vos ken bren-en un nisht oyf-hern?

וואס קען ברענען און נישט אויפהערן

Vos ken benk-en vé-nen on trern? *Refrain:*

וואס קען בענקען וויינען אן טרערן

Nar-ish-er bo-cher vos darí-stu fré-gn?

נארישער בחור וואס דארפסטו פרעגן

A shtén ken vak-sn vak-sn on ré-gn

א שטיין קען וואקסן, וואקסן אן רעגן

Li-be ken brene-n un nisht oif-hern

ליבע קען ברענען און נישט אויפהערן

A harts ken benk-en vé-nen on trern *Refrain:*

א הארץ קען בענקען וויינען אן טרערן

All night long a young man worries which girl to marry without embarrasing another one. "Young lady can you tell me what grows without rain, what yearns without tears, what can burn forever?" "Silly lad, a stone can grow without rain, a heart can yearn without tears and love can burn forever."

Rozhinkes Mit Mandlen

Moderately

In dem Bés Ha - mik - dosh in a vin - kel ché - der

zitst di al - mo - no bas Tsi - yon a - lén ir ben yo - chid - 'l

Yid - e - le vigt zi k' - sé - der un zingt im tsum shlof - n a

li - de - le shén ai - lu - lu - lu Un - ter Yid - e - les

vi - ge - le_____ shtét a klor vai - se tsi - ge - le_____

___ dos tsi - ge - le iz ge - for - en hand - len_____

dos vet zain dain be - ruf_____ ro - zhin -

kes____ mit mand - len_____ shlof - zhe Yid - e - le

shlof (hum) mm mm mm mm mm mm mm mm shlof ai - lu - lu

162

In dem bés-hamik-dosh	אין דעם בית המקדש
In a vin-kl ché-der	אין א ווינקל חדר
Zitst di al-mo-no Bas Tsi-yon a-lén	זיצט די אַלמנה בַת ציון אליין
Ir ben-yo-chidl Yid-e-le	איהר בֶּן-יָחידיל אידעלע
Vigt zi k'sé-der	וויגט זי כסדר
Un zingt im tsum shlo-ín	און זינגט איהם צום שלאפן
A li-de-le shén	א לידעלע שיין
Ai-lu-lu-lu	אי-לו-לו-לו
Un-ter Yi-de-les vi-gele	אונטער אידעלעס וויגעלע
Shtét a klor-vais tsi-ge-le	שטייט א קלאר ווייס ציגעלע
Dos tsi-ge-le iz ge-forn hand-len	דאס ציגעלע איז געפארן האנדלען
Dos vet zain dain ba-ruf	דאס וועט זיין דיין באַרוף
Rozh-in-kes mit mand-len	ראזשינקעס מיט מאַנדלען
Shlof zhe Yi-de-le shlof	שלאף זשע אידעלע שלאף

In a corner of the Temple the widowed daughter of Zion sits, rocking her only son, Yidele, to sleep. She sings him a tender lullaby about a snow white kid. The kid has been to market. That will be Yidele's calling too—trading in raisins and almonds.

This exquisite lullaby, long a favorite of Yiddish singers, first appeared in the opera *Shulamis* (1880) written by Abraham Goldfaden (1840-1908), the founder of the modern Yiddish Theater. The refrain of *Rozhinkes Mit Mandlen* is an adaptation of a well-known Yiddish folksong, *Unter Yankele's Vigele* (Beneath Yankel's Cradle).

Eli Eli

Eli Eli is a remarkable example of the evolution of a Yiddish theatrical ballad into a religious arietta. It became the signature song of Cantor Yossele Rosenblatt on his vaudeville tours around North America. The song, by Peretz Sandler, was written for a historical drama, *The Jewish King of Poland for a Night*, and was sung by Sophie Karp in her role as a Jewish girl about to be martyred for her faith. An immediate success, the song was performed by a succession of female performers. Over the decades, *Eli Eli* was printed in dozens of arrangements, and received national and then international recognition, but there was no mention of Sandler's name. The choral concert-style arrangments published by G. Schirmer and Carl Fischer gave no composer credit.

In 1919, Sandler began years of legal proceedings to have this song recognized as his own and published the song under his name. *Eli Eli* also reached Tin Pan Alley in several forms and Sandler heard it sung by Sophie Braslau on the stage of the Metropolitan Opera House. The acclaimed violinist, Mischa Elman, performed a new arrangement of Eli Eli in Carnegie Hall. In 1923 Sandler sued Joseph P. Katz, the company standing in for all other publishers. The case, on appeal, finally reached the United States Federal Court. A judicial ruling was published in full detail in the *New York Law Journal* of September 22, 1925. The decision was that "long delay in asserting authorship to a song, which is meanwhile being openly published and sold by others, constitutes fatal acquiesence..." This particular ruling has become a textbook case study on music copyright law in America.

Sh'ma Yis-ra-él   A-do-noi E-lo-hé - nu   A - do-noi   e - chod

Eli Eli lo-mo a-zav-to-ni?	אֵלִי אֵלִי לָמָה עֲזַבְתָּנִי
In fa-yer un flam hot men undz ge-brent	אין פייער און פלאם האט מען אונז געברענט
I-ber-al ge-macht undz tsu shand un tsu shpot	איבעראל געמאכט אונז צו שאנד און צו שפאט
Doch op-tsu-ven-den hot undz ké-ner nisht ge-kent	דאך אפצו-ווענדען האט אונז קיינער ניט געקענט
Fun dir main Got un fun dain hé-lig-er To-ro	פון דיר מיין גאט מיט דיין הייליגער תורה
Fun dain ge-bot	פון דייך געבאט
Eli Eli lo-mo a-zav-to-ni?	אֵלִי אֵלִי לָמָה עֲזַבְתָּנִי
Tog un nacht nor ich tracht	טאג און נאכט נאר איך טראכט
Fun dir main Got	פון דיר מיין גאט
Ich hit mit mo-ro op dain To-ro	איך היט מיט מוֹרָא אפ דיין תּוֹרָה
Un dain ge-bot	און דיין געבאט
Re-te mich re-te mich fun ge-far	רעטע מיך אוי רעטע מיך פון געפאר
Vi a mol di o-vos fun bé-zn g'-zar	ווי א מאל די אָבוֹת פון בייזן גזר
Her main ge-bét un main ge-vén	הער מיין געבעט און מיין געווען
Hel-fn ken-stu doch nor a-lén	העלפען קענסטו דאך נאר אליין
Sh'-ma Yis-ro-él A-do-noi E-lo-hé-nu	שְׁמַע יִשְׂרָאֵל יְיָ אֱלֹהֵינוּ
A-do-noi e-chod	יְיָ אֶחָד

My God, why have you forsaken me? They burned us in fire and flames. Everywhere they shamed and mocked us. No one could turn us away from you, your holy Tora and commandment.

Ani Ma'amin

Lento religioso

A-ni ma-a-min be-e-mu-na sh'-lé-ma a-ni ma-a-min a-ni___ ma-a-min be-e-mu-na sh'-lé-ma b'-vi-at ha-ma-shi-ach b'-af al pi she-yit-ma-mé-a vi-at ha-ma-shi-ach a-ni ma-a-min im___ kol___ ze___ a-ni ma-a-min a-ni ma-a-min a-ni ma-a-min a-ni___ ma-a-min be-e-mu-na sh'-lé-ma b'-vi-at___ ha-ma-shi-ach b'-vi-at ha-ma-shi-ach a-ni ma-a-min v'-

A-ni ma-a-min be-e-mu-na sh'-lé-ma
B'-vi-at ha-ma-shi-ach
V'-af al pi she-yit-ma-mé-ha
Im kol ze a-ni ma-a-min

אֲנִי מַאֲמִין בֶּאֱמוּנָה שְׁלֵמָה
בְּבִיאַת הַמָּשִׁיחַ
וְאַף עַל פִּי שֶׁיִּתְמַהְמֵהַּ
עִם כָּל זֶה אֲנִי מַאֲמִין

I believe with perfect faith in the coming of the Messiah; and although
he may tarry, I believe.

Ani Ma'amin composed by the Hasidic singer-composer Azriel Dovid Fastag is the best known liturgical song to emerge from the Warsaw Ghetto. It is known that thousands of Jews sang this melody to the text of *Ani Ma'amin* (from Maimonides' *Thirteen Articles of Faith*) during the Holocaust.

167

Zol Shoin Kumen Di G'ulo

On-ge-zol-yet oi-fn har-tsn macht men a l'-cha-yim   אנגעזאליעט אויפן הארצן מאכט מען א לחיים

Oib der u-met lozt nit ru-en zing-en mir a lid   אויב דער אומעט לאזט ניט רוען זינגען מיר א ליד

Iz ni-to kain bi-sl bron-fn, lo-mir trink-en ma-yim   איז ניטא קיין ביסל בראנפן-לאמיר טרינקען מים

Ma-yim cha-yim iz doch cha-yim—vos darf noch der Yid?   מַיִם חַיִים איז דאך חַיִים-וואס דארף נאך א ייד

Refrain   רעפריין

Zol shoin ku-men di g'-u-lo   זאל שוין קומען די גְאוּלָה

Mo-shi-ach kumt shoin bald!   מָשִיחַ קומט שוין באלד

'S-iz a dor fun ku-lo cha-yov zait nit kain na-ro-nim   ס'איז א דור פון כַּלוֹ חַיָב זייט ניט קיין נַעֲרָנים

Un fun zin-di-kn Mo-shi-ach gi-cher ku-men vet!   און פון זינדיקן-משיח גיכער קומען וועט

Ach du Ta-te-le in himl 's-bé-tn b'-né rach-mo-nim   אך דו טאטעלע אין הימל ס'בעטן בני רַחֲמָנים

Zé Mo-shi-ach zol nit ku-men a bi-se-le tsu shpét *Refrain:*   זע משיח זאל ניט קומען א ביסעלע צו שפעט

'S-tan-tsn bé-mer in di vel-der shtern oi-fn hi-ml   ס'טאנצן ביימער איז די וועלדער שטערן אויפן הימל

Reb Yis-ro-él der m'-chu-tn drét zich in der mit   ר' ישראל דער מחותן דרייט זיך אין דער מיט

'S-vet zich oif-ve-kn Mo-shi-ach fun zain ti-fn dri-ml   ס'וועט זיך אייפוועקן משיח פון זיין טיפן דרימל

Ven er vet der-hern und-zer t'fi-lo-di-ke lid   *Refrain:*   ווען ער וועט דערהערן אונדזער תפילהדיקע ליד

Though our hearts are ever aching, we will lift our cups to life. If there is no brandy then water will have to do. Salvation will soon come! The Messiah is on his way!

After the liberation, Shmerke Kaczerginski, a poet and folk song collector, adapted the lyrics of *Zol Shoin Kumen Di G'ulo* to a melody by Rabbi Abraham Isaac Kook, the chief Rabbi of Israel before World War I. The song was of great significance to the survivors who tried to revitalize their lives after the Holocaust. Along with many other songs that Kaczerginski collected and preserved from the period, *Zol Shoin Kumen Di G'ulo* appeared in his volume, *Lider fun di Getos un Lagern* (Songs of the Ghettos and Concentration Camps).

Vi Ahin Zol Ich Gén

Der Yid_____ vert ge - yogt un ge - plogt_____ nisht
zi - cher_____ is far im yé - der tog_____ zain
lé - bn_____ iz a fin - ste - re nacht_____ zain
shtré - bn_____ alts far im iz far - macht_____ far -
lo - zn_____ bloiz mit son - im kain fraint_____ kain hof - nung
_____ on a zi - che - m haint_____ Vi a - hin zol ich gén_____
_____ ver kon ent - fe - rn mir_____ vi a - hin zol ich gén_____
_____ az far - shlo - sn 'zyé - de tir_____ s'iz di velt grois ge - nug_____

nor far mir iz eng un klén_____ vi a blik ch'muz tsu - rik s'is tsu-shtert yé - de

brik vi a-hin zol ich gén_____ vi a-hin zol ich brik vi a-hin zol ich gén

©by J.J. Kammen Music

Der Yid vert ge-yogt un ge-plogt

Nisht zi-cher iz far im yéder tog

Zain le-bn iz a fins-te-re nacht

Kain shtré-bn alts far im iz far-macht

Far-lo-zn bloiz mit son-im kain fraint

Kain hof-nung on a zi-che-rn haint

Vi a-hin zol ich gén

Ver kon ent-fern mir

Vi a-hin zol ich gén

Az far-shlo-sn iz yéde tir

'Siz di velt grois ge-nug

Nor far mir iz eng un klén

Vi a blik 'ch-muz tsu-rik

'S-iz tsu-shtert yé-de brik

Vi a-hin zol ich gén

דער איד ווערט געיאגט און געפלאגט

נישט זיכער איז פאר אים יעדער טאג

זיין לעבן איז א פינסטערע נאכט

קיין שטרעבן אלץ פאר אים איז פארמאכט

פארלאזן בלויז מיט שונאים קיין פריינט

קיין האפנונג אן א זיכערן היינט

ווי אהין זאל איך גיין!

ווער קאן ענטפערן מיר

ווי אהין זאל איך גיין

אז פארשלאסן איז יעדע טיר

ס'איז די וועלט גרויס גענוג

נאר פאר מיר איז ענג און קליין

ווי א בליק כ'מוז צוריק

ס'איז צושטערט יעדע בריק

ווי אהין זאל איך גיין

Singable English

Tell me where can I go, there's no place I can see

Where to go, where to go, every door is closed to me

To the left to the right, it's the same in every land

There's nowhere to go, and it's me who should know

Wont you please understand

Now I know where to go, where my folks proudly stand

Let me go, let me go, to that precious promised land

No more left, no more right, lift your head for there is light

I am proud can't you see for at last I am free

No more wandering for me!

Written before World War II, *Vi Ahin Zol Ich Gén* was popular in the ghettos and D.P. camps. The lyrics are attributed to S. Korntayer, a Yiddish actor who died in the Warsaw ghetto in 1942.

Zog Nit Kénmol

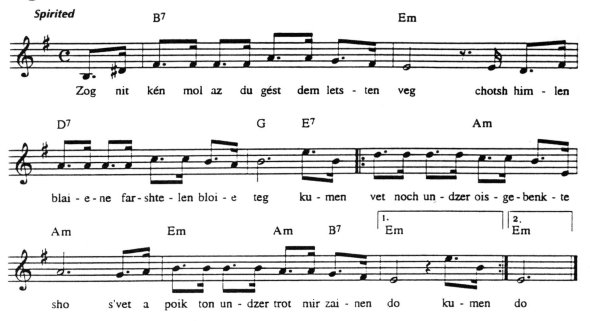

Zog nit kén-mol az du gést dem lets-tn veg
Chotsh him-len bla-ye-ne far-shte-ln blo-ye teg
Ku-men vet noch un-dzer ois-ge-benk-te sho
S'vet a poik ton und-zer trot— mir zain-en do!

Fun grin-empal-men-land biz vaisn land fun shné
Mir ku-men on mit und-zer pain mit und-zer vé
Un vu ge-fa-ln s'iz a shprits fun und-zer blut
Shpro-tsn vet dort und-zer g'-vu-ro und-zer mut

S-'vet di mor-gn zun ba-gil-dn undz dem haint
Un der nech-tn vet far-shvin-dn mi-tn faind
Nor oib far-zam-en vet di zun in dem ka-yor
Vi a pa-rol zol gén dos lid fun dor tsu dor

Dos lid ge-shri-bn iz mit blut un nit mit blai
S'iz nit kén li-dl fun a foi-gl oif der frai
Dos hot a folk tsvi-shn faln-di-ke vent
Dos lid ge-zung-en mit na-gan-es in di hent!

זאג ניט קיין מאל אז דו גייסט דעם לעצטן וועג
כאטש הימלען בלייענע פארשטעלן בלויע טעג
קומען וועט נאך אונדזער אויסגעבענקטע שעה
ס'וועט א פויק טאן אונדזער טראט -מיר זיינען דא!

פון גרינעם פאלמענלאנד ביז ווייסן לאנד פון שניי
מיר קומען אן מיט אונדזער פיין מיט אונדזער ווײ
און ווו געפאלן ס'איז א שפריץ פון אונדזער בלוט
שפראצן וועט דארט אונדזער גבורה אונדזער מוט

ס'וועט די מארגן זון באגילדן אונדז דעם היינט
און דער נעכטן וועט פארשווינדן מיטן פיינד
נאר אויב פארזאמען וועט די זון אין דעם קאיאר-
ווי א פאראל זאל גיין דאס ליד פון דור צו דור

דאס ליד געשריבן איז מיט בלוט און ניט מיט בליי
ס'איז ניט קיין לידל פון א פויגל אויף דער פריי
דאס האט א פאלק צווישן פאלנדיקע ווענט
דאס ליד געזונגען מיט נאגאנעס אין די הענט

Never say that you have reached your journey's end; that heavy clouds conceal the light of day. Upon us yet will dawn the day for which we yearn. Our tramping feet will then proclaim that we are here.

This song of the Jew's eternal faith was composed by Dmitri Pokrass and set to a poem of Hirsh Glick (1922-1944). *Zog Nit Kénmol* became the hymn of the United Partisan Organization in 1943, and spread to all the concentration camps and later to Jewish communities the world over.

ISRAELI MUSIC

Beginning with the last decade of the 19th century, a distinctive folk song was created that reflected the emergence of the modern Zionist movement. Though the origins of these folk song were based primarily on motifs and lyrics of the Diaspora, they were a unique form of folk music expression. For the most part those Jews who had always lived in the area of Palestine were religious scholars, pilgrims or members of centuries-old enclaves of Oriental/Near Eastern Jewish groups. Starting in 1882, modern Zionists came to rebuild the Jewish homeland and work on the land itself. Much of their song repertoire consisted of Eastern European Yiddish songs written by such composers as Abraham Goldfaden and Mark Warshawsky.

The Second *Aliyah* beginning in 1904 lasted until the outbreak of World War I in 1914. The settlers called themselves *chalutsim* (pioneers) and their songs were fashioned with Yiddish or Hebrew lyrics adapted to Slavic march tunes and Hasidic melodies. The Third *Aliyah* took place between 1918 and 1923 and thirty-five thousand Jews emigrated from Poland and Russia. Although their songs were still melodically rooted in Hasidic and Yiddish melodies, more of them were set to Hebrew lyrics.

Among the settlers dancing became an important and spirited activity. The dancers adapted Slavic and other East European dances in combination with those found among Arabs and Oriental/Near Eastern Jews and there were newly created tunes to serve as vehicles for dancing. One circle dance known as the *hora* (also the Rumanian name for a similar dance) rapidly became popular and achieved the status of a "national dance."

A fourth *Aliyah* 1924-1932 brought almost 100,000 immigrants to Palestine and this was a period of rich folk music. The subject of these songs was the beauty of the landscape and the pristine countryside. These songs easily carried over to the Diaspora, where Jews began to sing them with heartfelt expression.

The fifth *Aliyah* which began in 1933 and ended with the outbreak of World-War II brought 210,000 people including many refugees fleeing Germany and Europe in advance of the Nazis. In 1936 the Palestine Philharmonic was established and a radio station *Kol Yisrael* (Voice of

Israel), was put into broadcast operation. Soon there was a legion of composers, performers, and educators along with publications, concerts, and music institutions.

In 1948 the State of Israel was established and much musical creativity and activity began. Israeli composers created works that have since become classics. World renowned conductors, instrumentalists and vocalists appeared on a regular basis with the Israel Philharmonic and, soon after, with newly established orchestras in Haifa and Jerusalem. Opera and musical theater, festivals of both classic, folk, Hasidic and Klezmer began to flourish Although some of the native, acclaimed artists including Itzhak Perlman, Daniel Barenboim, and Pinchas Zukerman live outside the country, they return to perform in Israel on a regular basis.

Hatikvah

Hatikvah was adopted as the Jewish national anthem at the 18th Zionist Congress in 1897. The *Hatikvah* melody is one of the "wandering melodies" common to many countries. These folk melodies also inspired composers such as Biedrich Smetana who used them for the thematic basis of the *Moldau*. Originally titled *Tikvateynu* (Our hope), its nine stanzas were written in 1878 by Naphtali Herz Imber (1856-1909) Credit for the musical setting is generally attributed to Samuel Cohen, an early pioneer settler. At the Declaration of State of Israel on May 14, 1948, it was sung by the entire assembly with the accompaniment of the Palestine Symphony Orchestra

175

Hava Nagila

Hava na-gi-la v'-nis-m'-cha
U-ru a-chim b'-lév sa-mé-ach

הָבָה נָגִילָה וְנִשְׂמְחָה
עוּרוּ אַחִים בְּלֵב שָׂמֵחַ

Come let us be glad and rejoice. Arise brethren, with a joyful heart.

Contrary to popular belief, *Hava Nagila* is not an Israeli tune but a *nigun* composed in the Hasidic court of Sadigora, Poland. Introduced in 1918 by Abraham Zvi Idelsohn who also authored its lyrics, *Hava Nagila*. has remained the most representative Israeli folksong.

Y'rushalayim Shel Zahav

With conviction

A - vir ha - rim tsa - lul ka - ya - yin v' - ré - ach o - ra -
nim ni - sa b' - ru - ach ha - ar - ba - yim im kol pa - a - mo -
nim uv - tar - dé - mat i - lan va - e - ven sh'vu - ya ba - cha - lo - ma ha -
ir a - sher ba - dad yo - she - vet u - v' - li - ba cho - ma Y' - ru - sha -
la - yim shel za - hav v' - shel n' - cho - shet v' - shel or ha - lo l' - chol shi -
ra - yich a - ni ki nor Y' - ru - sha - nor
ra - yich a - ni___ ki - nor___ ki - nor

*last time

A-vir ha-rim tsa-lul ka-ya-yin v'-ré-ach o-ra-nim   אֲוִיר הָרִים צָלוּל כַּיַּיִן וְרֵיחַ אֳרָנִים

Ni-sa b'-ru-ach ha-ar-ba-yim im kol pa-a-mo-nim   נִשָּׂא בְּרוּחַ הָעַרְבַּיִם עִם קוֹל פַּעֲמוֹנִים

Uv-tar-dé-mat i-lan va-e-ven sh'-vu-ya ba-cha-lo-ma   וּבְתַרְדֵּמַת אִילָן וָאֶבֶן שְׁבוּיָה בַּחֲלוֹמָה

Ha-ir a-sher ba-dad yo-she-vet u-v'-li-ba cho-ma   הָעִיר אֲשֶׁר בָּדָד יוֹשֶׁבֶת וּבְלִבָּהּ חוֹמָה

Refrain   פזמון

Y'-ru-sha-la-yim shel za-hav v'shel n'cho-shet v'shel or   יְרוּשָׁלַיִם שֶׁל זָהָב וְשֶׁל נְחֹשֶׁת וְשֶׁל אוֹר

Ha-lo l'chol shi-ra-yich a-ni ki-nor   הֲלֹא לְכָל שִׁירַיִךְ אֲנִי כִּנּוֹר

Cha-zar-nu el bo-rot ha-ma-yim la-shuk v'-la-ki-kar   חָזַרְנוּ אֶל בּוֹרוֹת הַמַּיִם לַשּׁוּק וְלַכִּכָּר

Sho-far ko-ré b'-har ha-ba-yit ba-ir ha-a-ti-ka   שׁוֹפָר קוֹרֵא בְּהַר הַבַּיִת בָּעִיר הָעַתִּיקָה

U-vam-a-rot a-sher ba-se-la al-fé shma-shot zor-chot   וּבַמְּעָרוֹת אֲשֶׁר בַּסֶּלַע אַלְפֵי שְׁמָשׁוֹת זוֹרְחוֹת

V'shuv né-réd el yam ha-me-lach b'-de-rech Y'-ri-cho   וְשׁוּב נֵרֵד אֶל יַם הַמֶּלַח בְּדֶרֶךְ יְרִיחוֹ   פזמון

Refrain

Ach b'-vo-i ha-yom la-shir lach   אַךְ בְּבוֹאִי הַיּוֹם לָשִׁיר לָךְ

V'-lach lik-shor k'ta-rim   וְלָךְ לִקְשׁוֹר כְּתָרִים

Ka-ton-ti mi-ts'-ir ba-na-yich   קָטֹנְתִּי מִצְּעִיר בָּנַיִךְ

U-mé-a-cha-ron ham-sho-r'-rim   וּמֵאַחֲרוֹן הַמְשׁוֹרְרִים

Ki shméch tso-rév et has-fa-ta-yim   כִּי שְׁמֵךְ צוֹרֵב אֶת הַשְּׂפָתַיִם

K'-n'-shi-kat sa-raf   כִּנְשִׁיקַת שָׂרָף

Im esh-ka-chéch Y'-ru-sha-la-yim   אִם אֶשְׁכָּחֵךְ יְרוּשָׁלַיִם

A-sher ku-la za-hav   אֲשֶׁר כֻּלָּהּ זָהָב

Refrain   פזמון

Jerusalem of gold, of copper and of light, I shall accompany all the songs dedicated to you.

Y'rushalayim Shel Zahav (*Jerusalem of Gold*) by Naomi Shemer, was the most widely heard Israeli song in the immediate aftermath of the Six-Day War in 1967. Introduced by the singer Shuli Natan at the yearly Song Festival presented as a climax to Israel Independence Day, the song was an immediate success. With the retaking of the old city of Jerusalem and the return of the sacred Western Wall a short time later, the haunting melody and emotion laden lyrics gained additional popularity. Within days following the Six-Day War the song was recorded by a number of artists both in Israel and the United States. *Jerusalem of Gold* has remained one of the best known songs in Jewish communities worldwide.

Tsena Tsena

Tsena, Tsena became a runaway international "hit" when recorded by the American folksingers, *The Weavers*, in the early 1950's. More than a million copies of this recording (flip side—*Irene Good Night*), with lyrics both in Hebrew and English, were sold, and the song was popular among Jews as well as Gentiles. Authorship to the song was claimed by both the Israeli composer, Issachar Meron, and an American composer, Julius Grossman. A United States court rulled that the first two parts of the melody were written by Meron while the third part was by Grossman. Credits appeared accordingly in printed editions of the song. A short time after the Pope visited Israel in 1965, a nun composed a hymn in commemoration of the event and adapted it to the melody of *Tsena Tsena*. Although the original lyrics dealt with young women and soldiers, the new lyrics were sung as a prayer in a different religion.

Allegro moderato

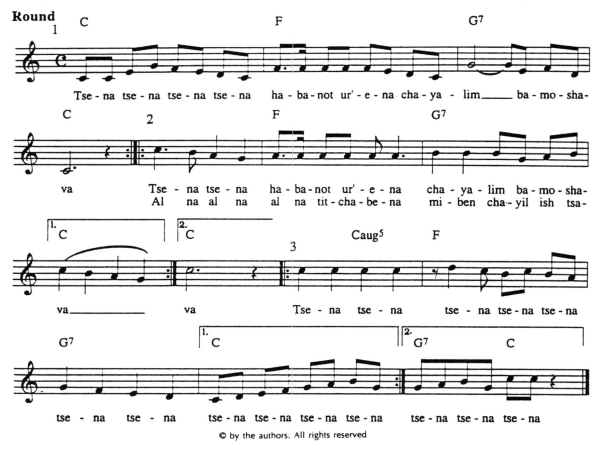

Tse-na ha-ba-not ur'-e-na
Cha-ya-lim ba-mo-sha-va
Al na tit-cha-be-na
Mi-ben cha-yil ish tsa-va

Come out, you fair girls, and greet the soldiers.
Do not fear the heroic warriors.

צֶאנָה הַבָּנוֹת וּרְאֶינָה
חַיָלִים בַּמוֹשָׁבָה
אַל נָא תִּתְחַבֶּנָה
מִבֶּן חַיִל אִישׁ צָבָא

179

Bashana Haba'a

Ba-sha-na ha-ba-a né-shév al ha-mir-pe-set
V'-nis-por tsi-po-rim no-d'-dot
Y'-la-dim ba-chuf-sha y'-sa-chak-u to-fe-set
Bén ha-ba-yit l'-vén ha-sa-dot
Refrain
Od tir-e, od tir-e
Ka-ma tov yi-ye
Ba-sha-na ha-ba-a

בַּשָּׁנָה הַבָּאָה נֵשֵׁב עַל הַמִּרְפֶּסֶת
וְנִסְפֹּר צִפֳּרִים נוֹדְדוֹת
יְלָדִים בַּחֻפְשָׁה יְשַׂחֲקוּ תּוֹפֶסֶת
בֵּין הַבַּיִת לְבֵין הַשָּׂדוֹת
פזמון
עוֹד תִּרְאֶה עוֹד תִּרְאֶה
כַּמָה טוֹב יִהְיֶה
בַּשָּׁנָה בַּשָּׁנָה הַבָּאָה

Next year, when peace will come, we shall return to the simple pleasures of life
so long denied us. You will see, you will see, O how good it will be next year!

First heard in 1969, *Bashana Haba'a* became an international favorite.
Versions appeared in many languages. *Bashana Haba'a's* popularity grew as
a result of its use as the background for El Al airline and the Israel Ministry of
Tourism commercials featured on American radio and television.

Erev Shel Shoshanim

Moderately

E - rev shel sho - sha - nim   ne - tsé   na el ha - bus - tan
mor b'-sa-mim u - l'- vo - na   l'-rag - léch mif - tan   lai - la yo - réd l'- at   v' -
ru - ach sho-shan nosh - va   ha - va el-chash lach shir ba - lat   ze - mer shel a - ha - va

E-rev shel sho-sha-nim né-tsé na el ha-bus-tan
Mor b'sa-mim u-l'vo-na l'-rag-léch mif-tan
Refrain
Lai-la yo-réd l'-at v'-ru-ach sho-shan nosh-va
Ha-va el-chash lach shir ba-lat ze-mer shel a-ha-va

Sha-char ho-ma yo-na ro-shéch ma-lé t'-la-lim
Pich el ha-bo-ker sho-sha-na ek-t'fe-nu li   *Refrain*

עֶרֶב שֶׁל שׁוֹשַׁנִים נֵצֵא נָא אֶל הַבּוּסְתָּן
מוֹר בְּשָׂמִים וּלְבוֹנָה לְרַגְלֵךְ מִפְתָּן
פזמון
לַיְלָה יוֹרֵד לְאַט וְרוּחַ שׁוֹשָׁן נוֹשְׁבָה
הָבָה אֶלְחַשׁ לָךְ שִׁיר בַּלָּאט זֶמֶר שֶׁל אַהֲבָה

שַׁחַר הוֹמָה יוֹנָה, רֹאשֵׁךְ מָלֵא טְלָלִים
פִּיךְ אֶל הַבֹּקֶר שׁוֹשַׁנָּה אֶקְטְפֶנּוּ לִי פזמון

An evening fragrant with roses. Let us go out to the orchard. Myrrh, spices and frankincense shall be as a threshold for your feet.

Although *Erev Shel Shoshanim* is often thought to be a folk tune, it is the best known song from the pen of the Israeli composer, Josef Hadar. In addition to its popularity in Jewish communities worldwide, it has become common practice in many synagogues to adapt this melody to sections of the *K'dusha* recited during Sabbath and festival morning services. *Erev Shel Shoshanim* is also used as a wedding ceremony processional.

Hakotel

D. Seltzer

Slowly with feeling

Am - da na - a - ra mul ha - ko - tel___ s'fa - ta - yim kér - va v' - san -

tér am - ra li t'ki - ot ha - sho - far cha - za - kot hén a - val ha - sh'ti - ka od yo -

tér am - ra li Tsi - yon har ha - ba - yit___ shat - ka li ha - g'mul v' - ha -

z'chut u - ma she - za - har al mits - cha bén ar - ba - yim ha - ya ar - ga - man shel mal -

chut ha - ko - tel_____ é - zov v' - a - tse - vet_____ ha -

ko - tel_____ o - fe - ret va - dam_____ yésh a - na - shim im lév shel

e - ven_____ yésh a - va - nim im lév a - dam_____

Am-da na-a-ra mul ha-ko-tel
S'-fa-ta-yim kér-va v'-san-tér
Am-ra li t'-ki-ot ha-sho-far cha-za-kot hén
A-val ha-sh'ti-ka od yo-tér
Am-ra li Tsi-yon har ha-ba-yit
Shat-ka li ha-g'mul v'-ha-z'chut
U-ma she-za-har al mits-cha bén ar-ba-yim
Ha-ya ar-ga-man shel mal-chut
Refrain
Ha-ko-tel é-zov v'-a-tse-vet
Ha-ko-tel o-fe-ret va-dam
Yésh a-na-shim im lév shel e-ven
Yésh a-na-shim im lév a-dam

A-mad ha-tsan-chan mul ha-ko-tel
Mi-kol mach-lak-to rak e-chad
A-mar li "la-ma-vet én d'-mut ach yésh ko-ter—
Tish-a mi-li-me-ter bil-vad"
A-mar li "é-ne-ni do-mé-a"
(V'shav l'-hash-pil ma-ba-tim)
"Ach sa-ba she-li E-lo-him ha-yo-dé-a
Ka-vur kan b'-har ha-zé-tim"
Refrain

Am-da bish-cho-rim mul ha-ko-tel
I-mo shel e-chad min ha-chir
Am-ra li "é-né na-a-ri ha-dol-kot hén
V'-lo ha-né-rot she-ba-kir"
Am-ra li "é-ne-ni ro-she-met
Shum pe-tek lit-mon bén s'-da-kav
Ki ma she-na-ta-ti la-ko-tel rak e-mesh
Ga-dol mi-mi-lim u-mich-tav"
Refrain

עָמְדָה נַעֲרָה מוּל הַכֹּתֶל
שְׂפָתַיִם קָרְבָה וְסַנְטֵר
אָמְרָה לִי תְּקִיעוֹת הַשּׁוֹפָר חֲזָקוֹת הֵן
אֲבָל הַשְּׁתִיקָה עוֹד יוֹתֵר
אָמְרָה לִי צִיּוֹן הַר הַבַּיִת
שָׁתְקָה לִי הַגְּמוּל וְהַזְכוּת
וּמַה שֶׁזָּהַר עַל מִצְחָהּ בֵּין עַרְבַּיִם
הָיָה אַרְגָּמָן שֶׁל מַלְכוּת
פזמון
הַכֹּתֶל אֵזוֹב וְעַצֶּבֶת
הַכֹּתֶל עוֹפֶרֶת וָדָם
יֵשׁ אֲנָשִׁים עִם לֵב שֶׁל אֶבֶן
יֵשׁ אֲבָנִים עִם לֵב אָדָם

עָמַד הַצַּנְחָן מוּל הַכֹּתֶל
מִכָּל מַחְלַקְתּוֹ רַק אֶחָד
אָמַר לִי לַמָּוֶת אֵין דְּמוּת אַךְ יֵשׁ קֹטֶר
תִּשְׁעָה מִלְמֶטֶר בִּלְבַד
אָמַר לִי אֵינֶנִּי דוֹמֵעַ
(וְשָׁב לְהַשְׁפִּיל מַבָּטִים)
אַךְ סַבָּא שֶׁלִּי אֱלֹהִים הַיּוֹדֵעַ
קָבוּר כָּאן בְּהַר הַזֵּיתִים
פזמון

עָמְדָה בִּשְׁחוֹרִים מוּל הַכֹּתֶל
אִמּוֹ שֶׁל אֶחָד מִן הַחַיי"ר
אָמְרָה לִי עֵינֵי נַעֲרִי הַדּוֹלְקוֹת הֵן
וְלֹא הַנֵּרוֹת שֶׁבַּקִּיר
אָמְרָה לִי אֵינֶנִּי רוֹשֶׁמֶת
שׁוּם פֶּתֶק לִטְמוֹן בֵּין סְדָקָיו
כִּי מַה שֶׁנָּתַתִּי לַכֹּתֶל רַק אֶמֶשׁ
גָּדוֹל מִמִּלִים וּמִכְתָּב
פזמון

A young girl, a paratrooper and a mother stand leaning against the Western Wall
each deep in thought. There are people with hearts of stone; there are stones
with human hearts.

Ose Shalom

O-se sha-lom bim-ro-mav
Hu ya-a-se sha-lom a-lé-nu
V'-al kol Yis-ra-él v'-im-ru a-mén

עֹשֶׂה שָׁלוֹם בִּמְרוֹמָיו
הוּא יַעֲשֶׂה שָׁלוֹם עָלֵינוּ
וְעַל כָּל יִשְׂרָאֵל וְאָמְרוּ אָמֵן

May He who makes peace in the high places make peace for Israel and
for all mankind and say Amen.

Ose Shalom with text from the prayer book was introduced at the first Israeli
Hasidic Song Festival in 1969. It quickly became one of Israel's most popular
songs and spread to many Jewish communities. *Ose Shalom* is sung during
Sabbath and festivals sevices in many synagogues worldwide

Hal'luya

K. Oshrat & S. Or

Ha-l'-lu-ya la-o-lam   הַלְלוּיָה לָעוֹלָם

Ha-l'-lu-ya ya-shi-ru ku-lam   הַלְלוּיָה יָשִׁירוּ כֻּלָם

B'-mi-la a-chat bo-dé-da   בְּמִלָה אַחַת בּוֹדְדָה

Ha-lév ma-lé b'-ha-mon to-da   הַלֵב מָלֵא בַּהֲמוֹן תּוֹדָה

V'-ho-lém gam hu é-ze o-lam nif-la   וְהוֹלֵם גַם הוּא אֵיזֶה עוֹלָם נִפְלָא

Ha-l'-lu-ya im ha-shir   וַהַלְלוּיָה עִם הַשִׁיר

Ha-l'-lu-ya al yom she-mé-ir   הַלְלוּיָה עַל יוֹם שֶׁמֵאִיר

Ha-l'-lu-ya al ma she-ha-ya   הַלְלוּיָה עַל מַה שֶׁהָיָה

U-ma she-od lo ha-ya   וּמַה שֶׁעוֹד לֹא הָיָה

Ha-l'-lu-ya   הַלְלוּיָה

Sing Haleluya to the world. Sing Haleluya to a bright new day. Haleluya
for that which was–and for all that will be. Haleluya!

This was the winning song in the 1979 *Eurovision Song Festival*. *Hal'luya* was recorded in an
English version by Steve Lawrence and Eydie Gorme under the name of "Parker and Penny."

IV

APPENDIX

BAKASHOT

While the Ashkenazic world was developing its synagogue and secular music, the Sephardic and Oriental communities were composing their own liturgical and para-liturgical songs. Due to the influence of the *Zohar* (The Book of Splendor) and the Kabbalists in Safed, rising at midnight to sing became very popular. In a volume, *Shivchei Ha-ari* the following is related

> And Rabbi Abraham Halevy (who settled in Jerusalem in approximately 1515), would rise at midnight every night to go from street to street and weep in a loud voice and shout aloud in harsh wailing tones....calling each scholar by name and would not leave him until he saw him rise from his bed....and at the same hour they would all rise to go to the synagogues and houses of learning and would chant the *tikun chatsot* (the midnight vigils) and then would study, each man according to his understanding.

Some groups would study the *Zohar* and the *Kabbalah* and some the *Talmud, Mishna* or the Bible, and then they would sing hymns from the Psalms and refrains and *Bakashot* (songs of supplication) until the light of the day. Influenced by Hayim Vital, a pupil of the *Ari*, and by the Kabbalists, associations were formed in both the East and the West that instituted customs such as *tikun chatsot, shirat t'hilim* (singing psalms), singing *bakashot* and other prayers. The great importance the mystics attributed to singing from midnight on led to the establishment of *Shomrim Laboker*, choral groups of early risers.

Much poetry was needed in order to supply these groups, and poets were encouraged to fulfill the need by writing. The *Bakashot* were developed in a sophisticated manner, particularly in two major centers, Syria and Morocco. On Sabbath eve, in the wintertime between *Sukot* and *Pesach*, men, women and children would go to the synagogue after midnight and spend the entire *ashmoret sh'lisheet* (third watch) in solo and choral singing until daybreak. From Morocco and Syria this custom spread to many other places and the singing of *Bakashot* is still observed in Oriental Jewish communities.

THE YEMENITE *DIWAN*

The *Diwan* is a collection of songs sung by Yemenite men for weddings, circumcisions, the Sabbath, and holy days. Unlike the special *piyut* of the Jews of Morocco and Syria that were meant only for the *Bakashot*, the *Diwan* includes all types of songs accepted by Yemenite Jews. The material included in the *Diwan* is meant to be sung and even to be accompanied by dancing. In addition, unlike other *diwans*, or collections of Spanish songs that are widespread in the East, the Yemenite *Diwan* contains no instructions as to the melody to be used or the way in which the song should be performed. Before the *Diwan* appeared, many of the special occasion songs popular in the Yemenite community were those written by Spanish poets. Because of the increase in the poetic output of native Yemenite Jews, their work was included in the prayer books along with the classical Spanish *piyut*.

The earliest known copy of the *Diwan* appeared during the time of Shalom Shabazi (1619-1680), regarded as the greatest Yemenite Jewish poet. Many of his poems are included in the *Diwan*. Shabazi was the first to add a body of general songs to the existing body of nuptial songs. These were introduced and sung at the wedding ceremonies. Themes of dispersion and redemption, the main subjects of poems written by Yemenite Jews for many generations, were introduced into wedding songs. Although the *Diwan* contains a number of poems that are sung in the synagogue, most of its contents are intended for festive occasions and, in some cases, as accompaniment to dancing.

189

A Sabbath hymn from the Diwan

BADCHONIM

Although instrumental music and secular song were prohibited in Israel after the destruction of the Temple in Jerusalem, both were permitted at weddings and on Purim. It was even considered a *mitsva* to sing, dance and make merry in order to cheer the bride by praising her beauty and talents. Prominent Talmudists did not consider it beneath their dignity to dance before the bride with a palm-branch in hand singing the refrain *kala na'a vachasuda* (O, beautiful and virtuous bride). The disciples of Hillel often suspended their study in order to dance at weddings in the presence of the bride.

It is most likely that Jewish people seized this opportunity for rejoicing in order to give vent to their suppressed longing for music, song and dance. The spiritual leaders found it difficult to check this passion, and tried to direct the singers and the merry-makers to songs of religious and ethical content. The singers and merry-makers, therefore, used to interweave their couplets and jingles with Biblical phrases and Talmudic sayings.

The professional *badchonim* (marriage entertainers) can be found as far back as the early centuries of the Common Era, and they remained an integral part of Jewish weddings throughout the Diaspora. It was their task to cheer those who were sad and to make peace between dissident factions in both the family and community. They sought to elevate and instruct the masses while entertaining them through witty and subtle satire. The *badchonim* created their songs extemporaneously according to the particular conditions they encountered at each wedding. By the 16th century, the Jewish wedding featured the *badchen* along with the jester and clowns whose repertoire included humorous, light, often bawdy songs, as well as instrumental and acrobatic antics, dances and even small dramatic presentations. The *badchen*, on the other hand, delivered the more serious discourses, together with the rabbi and the bridegroom. Gradually, both types of entertainment became intertwined, and, by the 19th century, the *badchen* were performing in a manner and with a repertoire which combined the art of all the wedding entertainers.

The *badchonim* were not solely merry-makers and jesters. Many would mingle tears with the cup of joy that they presented to the young couples and the wedding guests. Even at this happiest of occasions, the *badchonim* used the opportunity to remind the wedding guests, as well as bride and bridegroom, of the trials and tribulations of the Jews in the Diaspora. The *badchen*, who was seen as a true son of the Jewish people, accomplished this with a tone of love.

In addition to the Jewish wedding, *badchonim* took part in song, merry-making and rejoicing on Purim. As far back as the Talmudic times levity was permitted on this joyous holiday. The celebration consisted of special humorous Purim songs in the language of each country. Many of these songs are retained, in the Judeo Italian, Judeo-Spanish and Judeo-German repertoire. The Purim festivities brought about the creation of the Jewish folk-comedies. While dramatic performance was usually considered frivolous, an exception was made with regard to Purim. In *Gaonic* times, the dramatization of the story of Esther was a well-established custom among the Jews in the Orient. Similar dramatizations are reported in other countries during the Middle Ages. The real Purim play, however, the Judeo-German *Purimspiel*, did not make its appearance until the first decade of the 18th century. The *Purimspiel* was the forerunner of the Jewish Theater.

A klezmer group and badchen (third from right) White Russia late 1900's.

KLEZMORIM

After the destruction of the Second Temple in Jerusalem, instrumental music was prohibited except for weddings. Making music for Gentiles was allowed, however, for those poor Jews who earned their livelihood in this manner. Instrumental music was also allowed at the dedication of a synagogue or Torah scroll. In the Oriental Jewish communities, hymns with musical accompaniment were sung in synagogues during the intermediate days of *Pesach* (Passover) and *Sukot*. Musical instruments were also allowed to be played in the *sukahs* of various Hasidic courts during the intermediate days of the holiday. This custom was already in place during the 12th century and has continued into modern times.

During the Middle Ages, music making became a standard profession among the Jews in the Orient as well as in Europe. There were *klezmorim* in almost every city. History records famous individuals who served as court musicians to sultans, caliphs, dukes, kings and even popes. In some places the Jewish musicians were the primary music suppliers and performed even in Christian religious ceremonies.

Klezmer is a contraction and slight corruption of the Hebrew words *kley zemer* (musical instruments) and became the Yiddish name for a small popular orchestra. As far back as the 15th century there were music ensembles that traveled from place to place performing for Christian as well as Jewish events and celebrations. Members of these bands had no formal music education but were blessed with natural musicianship. They played Jewish style and popular Gentile tunes as well. The *klezmer* were capable of creating, improvising and incorporating newly adapted styles into their existing repertory.

The *klezmorim* in Central and Eastern Europe were the forerunners of a host of musicians of Jewish extraction, both composers and performers, who, from the beginning of the 19th century, contributed enormously toward the building of European art music. At the end of the 19th century, a number of *klezmer* left Eastern Europe for the United States where they continued their musical activities within the Jewish community.

Klezmorim, drawing by Leonid Pasternak, Prague, 1901

A Klezmer ensemble in Galicia

The most popular Jewish milieu for the *klezmer* was the wedding. Here the instrumentalist could interact closely with members of his community. The *klezmer* played a specifically Jewish wedding repertoire in addition to local peasant dance tunes. Literally every step of the way was accompanied by the *klezmer*. From the *chosnmol* (a pre-wedding party sponsored by the bridegroom), to the *sheva brachot* (the post wedding parties), specific dances were played for members of the family, friends and guests. Some of the wedding dances included the *broygez tantz* (dance of anger), *patsh tantz* (hand clapping dance) marches, *chosidls, horas, shers* and *doinas*.

In the 1970's the word *klezmer* was re-introduced by Giora Feidman, an Argentine born seventh generation *klezmer*, who had emigrated to Israel and became the principle clarinetist of the Israel Philharmonic Orchestra. After playing under the baton of Zubin Mehta for a number of years, he began to concertize world-wide bringing Jewish music to large enthusiastic audiences, both Jewish and Gentile. In 1980, the first re-issue of period 78 vinyl recordings titled *Klezmer Music 1910-1942* was released. This was followed several years later by the re-issue, *Klezmer Music 1910-1926*. A significant occurrence was the inclusion of *Kapelye*, one of the first of the revivalist Klezmer bands, in the Hollywood movie, *The Chosen.* In 1984, the New York based *Kapelye*, led by Henry Sapoznik, became the first American klezmer band to tour and perform in Europe. Word began to filter through that this music was receiving warm reception throughout the United States and klezmer groups began to form in American cities including Seattle, Albuquerque, New Orleans, Boston, Chicago, Boulder, Portland and many others.

By the end of the 20th century, atypical Jewish music styles were added to the presentation, including jazz, bluegrass, blues, country etc.

CONGREGATIONAL SINGING

From the last decade of the 19thcentury and well into and the first two decades of the 20th century, the larger more established Orthodox, Reform and Conservative synagogues continued to employ cantors and professional choirs. many congregants however, felt that they did not need to be "sung down to" by virtuoso performers and choirs with their often long, drawn out liturgical recitatives and choral compositions. Outside the synagogue service such renditions were acceptable and Jews flocked in throngs to popular events featuring cantorial "stars" and their musical interpretations of the liturgy.

In the late 1920's a radical concept, congregational singing, was introduced into a fledgling group of Orthodox synagogues. Although a number of melodies had in the past been adapted in Hasidic synagogues to such Sabbath liturgical texts as *L'cho Dodi*, *El Odon* and *Mimkomcho*, community singing during services was kept to a minimum. The Orthodox synagogues, in their musical "reform," no longer hired professional cantors or choirs but encouraged their able congregants to be *baale t'filoh* and conduct services. These *baale t'filoh* set melodies, to the liturgy and many of them spread to other congregations and became standard.

Large, Modern Orthodox Synagogues began to proliferate throughout the United States, Canada and, after the Israel War of Independence, also in Israel. The Conservative Movement also turned to congregational singing but unlike the Modern Orthodox, their synagogues were still served by professional cantors. Although professional cantors, cantorial soloists and choirs continued in the Reform Movement synagogues, congregational singing became an important aspect of its prayer service.

The congregational melodies consisted of Hasidic *nigunim*, Yiddish folk songs, and early 20th century secular pioneer melodies from Palestine. In addition, melodies of the great 19th century composers, Sulzer and Lewandowski were utilized. The metrical poetry rather than the recitative portions of the liturgy were the most musically adaptable. During the latter part of the twentieth century, *Havurot*, *Renewal and Healing* services appeared with increased frequency and many of their melodies were created by contemporary artists including Debbie Friedman, Craig Taubman and Michael Isaacson. Since the death of Rabbi Carlebach in 1994, the *Carlebach Minyan* has grown and attracted thousands of individuals. These services feature the music of the famous rabbi almost exclusively.

NEO-HASIDIC SONG AND YESHIVA MELODIES

During the 1960's a new style of Hasidic song developed in the United States. Because it did not adhere strictly to the melodic or rhythmic characteristics of Hasidic songs, many traditionalists felt that that this type of music could, at best, be labeled *shir dati* (religious song) or neo-Hasidic.

Most prominent among the new songwriters was the Berlin born, American ordained, Rabbi Shlomo Carlebach. His first of many recordings, *Han'shomo Loch* (1961), was highly successful with a large segment of American Jewish youth. In addition to the contemporary sound of the melodies, the recording featured choral and instrumental arrangements by Milt Okun, well known musician active in the American music.field. The resulting musical flavor was perceptibly different from that which had heretofore been considered "Jewish."

To Carlebach also belongs the distinction of being first in taking the *nigun* out of its usual habitats—the synagogue, the *farbrengen* (Hassidic gatherings), weddings and bar-mitzvahs, and to present it in concert accompanied by musical instruments. He was followed by the Rabbis' Sons, a group of four Orthodox young men trained in American yeshivas. The Rabbis' Sons appeared in many major cities during the late 1960's and early 1970's and the influence of contemporary American music was evident in their repertoire.

The public performances of Shlomo Carlebach and the Rabbis' Sons laid the groundwork for other concertizing groups and many phonograph recordings. These groups featured new melodies set to liturgical texts from the *Siddur* (prayerbook), the Psalms and the Bible. The widest recognition of this newer music may be attributed to the first *Chassidic Song Festival* presented in Israel during November of 1969. Held as an open competition, the Festival was later featured in several major Israeli cities and the recording of the initial performance became a world wide success. The subsequent yearly festivals and their recordings as well as the appearance of the troupe before Jewish audiences world-wide, gave Hassidic music a new image.

However, many music purists nurtured on the melodies of Modzitz, Bobov, Lubavitch, Ger, Vishnitz and other Hassidic dynasties, were slow in accepting these new melodies. In addition, the commercialization of this material in staged performance with singers, orchestra, and costumed childrens' choirs left many disenchanted. The proliferation of phonograph recordings, cassettes and most recently compact discs created a transitory "Hasidic Hit Parade" in which melodies became popular only to be replaced by newer melodies a short time later.

Nevertheless, much of this music has become mainstream, even among the traditionalists. Mordechai Ben David and Avrham Fried, to name just two of the more prominent artists, have become household names in Orthodox circles. Their recordings are popular even among secular Jews and the melodies they introduced have become part of the Jewish musical repertoire.

Bilvavi

S. Brazil

THE VALUE OF SONG

From the writings and sayings of the Hassidic leaders come these statements regarding the unique power of *neginah* (song).

Of all the halls of heaven, the hall of music is the lowest and the smallest, but he who wants to approach God, has only to enter this hall.
—Rabbi Uri of Strelisk, *The Seraph*

How do you pray to the Lord? Is it possible to pray to the Lord with words alone? Come, I will show you a new way to the Lord – not with words or sayings but with song. We will sing, and the Lord on high will understand us.
—Rabbi Nachman of Bratslav

The tongue is the pen of the heart, but melody is the quill of the soul.
—Rabbi Shneur Zalman

Every locksmith has a master key with which he can open many doors. *Neginah* is such a key, for it can unlock all doors.
—Sayings of Chabad

Speech reveals the thought of the mind, but melody reveals the emotions of longing and delight. These stem from the inner self, from the very soul, and are much higher than reason and intellect.
—Rabbi Yosef Yitschok of Lubavitch

A person should not have an ear just to hear songs of others, but also to hear the songs which sing from within his heart.
—Rabbi Yisroel of Modzitz

Through the power of *neginah* one may conquer the heart.
—Maggid of Koznitz

Through song the gates of heaven can be opened. Sadness closes them. The origin of all songs is holy, for impurity has no song. It is the root of all sadness.
—Rabbi Naftoli of Ropshitz

One *nigun* can express more than a thousand words.
—Tsadik of Kuzmir

Even the most wicked can be turned to repentance upon hearing a song which emanates from a *Tsadik's* innermost heart.
—Baal Shem Tov

Our opponents wonder at the sight of Hassidim singing and dancing at their assemblies. If they understood our viewpoint, would they not become our comrades?
—Sudilkover Rebbe

In reality, for those who understand that which they hear, a song tells more than a story.
—Rabbi Shneur Zalman

Every science, every religion, every philosophy has a pattern of song. The higher the religion or science, the more exalted its music.
—Rabbi Nachman of Bratslav

Music opens a window to the secret places of the soul.
— Sayings of Chabad

It is said that the "Mansion of Song" and the "Mansion of Penitence" are close to each other, and I say that the "Mansion of Song" is the "Mansion of Penitence."
—Rabbi Yisroel of Modzitz

Many a melody once chanted by the Levites in the holy Temple is now in exile among the unlearned common people.
—Rabbi Isaac of Kalev

He who has no feeling for *neginah* has no feeling for Hasidism. He who has a great feeling for *neginah* has a great feeling for Hasidism
—Rabbi Isaac of Kalev

Rejoice that you have an opportunity to sing unto God.
—Rabbi Mendel of Vitebsk

When I hear a song from the mouth of a Jew, I can ascertain how much fear of God there is within him and whether he is wise or foolish.
—Rabbi Yisroel of Modzitz

Melody is the outpouring of the soul. Words interrupt the stream of emotions. For the songs of the souls, at the time they are swaying in the high regions to drink from the well of the Almighty King, consist of tones only, dismantled of words.
—Rabbi Shneur Zalman

Were I blessed with a sweet voice, I could sing you new hymns and songs every day, for with the daily rejuvenation of the world, new songs are created.
—Rabbi of Ger

Song is the revelation of higher beauty, but *séder* (form) in song is beauty proper at its highest peak.
—Rabbi Yosef Yitschok of Lubavitch

If I were a singer, I would accept upon myself the duty of traveling from city to city in order to lead services in the various synagogues.
—Rabbi Pinchas of Koretz

A person sees himself as he truly is through a Hasidic *nigun*.
—Sayings of Chabad

Song opens a gate from the mind to the heart.
—Sayings of Chabad

Music originates from the prophetic spirit, and has the power to elevate one to prophetic inspiration.
—Rabbi Nachman of Bratslav

In all *nigunim* can be found love and fear of the Lord.
—Rabbi Nachman of Bratslav

The nature of the Levites' work was the daily creation of new songs. Also the angels on high create new songs daily, and with the power of the new song they renew each day the miracle of Creation.
—Rabbi Pinchas of Koretz

The bad traits in man come from the animal instinct within him. Through the power of the *nigun* it is possible to remove this instinct.
—Baal Shem Tov

All the work of the angels is performed with song.
—Rabbi Nachman of Bratslav

I cannot sit at the Sabbath table without a new song. There is no festive Shabbath without a new song.
—Tsadik of Kuzmir

He who does not spring from the "Mansion of Song" to the "Mansion of Fear" (of the Lord) is a fool.
—Rabbi Naftoli of Ropshitz

A melody should be sung with the same correctness that one would employ in citing a commentary on Torah learned from one's teacher or rabbi.
—Rabbi Yosef Yitschok of Lubavitch

A *nigun* can pull one out of the deepest mire.
—Rabbi Shneur Zalman

When one hears a song sung well or played well, all sadness is driven away and is replaced with joy.
—Rabbi Nachman of Bratslav

Song reveals the beauty within the soul.
—Rabbi Sholem Duber of Lubavitch

Through song calamities can be removed.
—Rabbi Nachman of Bratslav

Songs heard at Hassidic gatherings arouse their listeners to repentance.
—Rabbi Shmuel of Lubavitch

Know that each shepherd has his own individual song characterized by the surroundings in which he tends his flock. For every blade of grass has its own melody, and from the combined melodies of all these blades comes the shepherd's own song.
—Rabbi Nachman of Bratslav

Neginah is the language of the soul.
—Rabbi Shneur Zalman

If you sing a *nigun* correctly without mistakes, then the nigun speaks for itself.
—Sayings of Chabad

Lord of the Universe, were I a singer I would not allow you to live in the heavens, but you would be forced to live with us here on earth.
—Rabbi Pinchas of Koretz

Song elevates an individual and brings him closer to God.
—Rabbi Shneur Zalman

Nigunim composed according to the rules of music are not truthful. These are songs that do not emanate from the heart.
—Tsadik of Kuzmir

SELECTED ARTISTS AND THEIR CONTRIBUTIONS
TO JEWISH MUSIC
A Partial Listing

Achron, Joseph 1886-1943 composer and violinist
Evening Service for the Sabbath (1932) *Hebraique Melody*
Golem

Algazi, Leon 1890-1971 conductor and writer
Chants Sephardis

Baer, Abraham 1834-1894 cantor and editor
Baal T'fillah

Binder, Abraham Wolfe 1895-1966
Selected Works: *Holy Land Impressions for Orchestra,*
Dybbuk Suite , *A Goat for Chelm*

Bayer, Bathia 1928 musicologist
The Material Relics of Music in Ancients Palestine and its
Environs , *The Biblical Nebel*

Birnbaum, Eduard 1855-1920 cantor and musicologist
The Birnbaum Collection

Dunajewski, Abraham 1843-1911 composer and conductor
Israelitische Tempel Compositionen (2 volumes)

Ellstein, Abraham 1907-1963 composer and pianist
Ode to the King of Kings, Negev Concerto

Ephros, Gershon 1890 cantor and composer
Cantorial Anthology

Freed, Isadore (1900-1960) composer, conductor and lecturer
Harmonizing the Jewish Modes

Gerovitsch, Eliezer 1844-1914 cantor and composer
Shire Tefillah (1890) *Shirei Simroh*

Geshuri, Meir 1897-1978 musicologist, writer
Encyclopedia of Hassidism: Hanigun V'Harikud Bachasidut
(Melody and Dance among Hasidim)

Gniessin, Michael 1883-1957 composer, teacher and writer
Operas the Youth of Abraham, The Maccabeans

Goldfarb, Israel 1879-1956 rabbi and cantor
*Song and Praise for Sabbath Eve, Synagogue Melodies
for the High Holidays*

Gradenwitz, Peter 1910 musicologist
*The Music of Israel — It's Rise and Growth through
5000 years*

Helfman, Max 1901-1963 composer, conductor and lecturer
Shabbat Kodesh

Holde, Artur 1885-1962 critic, conductor and writer
Jews in Music

Naumbourg, Samuel 1815-1880 Cantor and composer
Reediting Rossi's *Hashirim Asher Leshlomo*

Nowakowsky, David 1848-1921 choirmaster and composer
*Shire David — Kabbalath Shabbat,
Shire David — Tefilot Neilah*

Partos, Odeon 1907-1977 composer, teacher, violinist
Yizkor

Rabinovitch, Israel 1894-1963 editor and writer
Of Jewish Music — Ancient and Modern

Rubin, Ruth 1906-1999 researcher, author, singer
Voices of a People: The Story of Yiddish Folksong

Rumshinsky, Joseph 1881-1956 composer and conductor
Operettas: *Dem Rebbens Nigun. Tzubrochene Fiedele*

Secunda, Sholom 1894-1974 composer and conductor.
Yiddish Theater Operettas, Bai Mir Bistu Shén,

Sendry, Alfred 1884-1976 musicologist and conductor
*Bibliography of Jewish Music, Music in Ancient Israel
The Music of the Jews in the Diaspora*

Stutchewsky, Joachim 1891-1982 cellist, composer, writer
*Musical Folklore of Eastern European Jewry,
Haklezmorim*

Weiner Lazare 1897-1982 composer
The Golem (opera), *The Marred Passover* (ballet)
Chanson Hebraique (cello and piano)

Vinaver, Chemjo 1900-1974 choral, conductor and composer
Anthology of Jewish Music

Weisser, Albert 1918-1982 Musicologist and composer
The Modern Renaissance of Jewish Music,
Three Popular Songs after Sholom Aleichem

Weisser, Joshua 1888-1952 Cantor and composer
Shirei Beth Hakneseth

Werner, Eric 1901-1988 musicologist
The Sacred Bridge, A Voice Still Heard,
The Sacred Songs of the Ashkenazic Jews.

Zilberts, Zavel 1881-1949 choral director, composer
Havdala, The Complete High Holiday Liturgy for the Hazzan

Zunser, Eliakum 1836-1913 Eastern European Poet and Singer
Selected Songs of Eliakum Zunser

JEWISH ARTISTS
A Partial Listing

A leaf through the roster of Jewish conductors, composers, instrumentalists and musical entertainers of the 20th century, shows their number to be disproportionate to the Jewish population in the world. Although a number of these artists assimilated or converted during their careers, and did not contribute significantly to the body of Jewish music, their general musical accomplishments are truly noteworthy.

INSTRUMENTALISTS

Ashkenazy Vladimir 1937- (piano)
Bar Ilan David 1930- (piano)
Dichter Misha 1945- (piano)
Fleisher Leon 1928- (piano)
Goodman Benny 1909-1986 (clarinet)
Heifetz Jascha 1901-1987 (violin)
Hess, Myra 1890-1965 (piano)
Horowitz Vladimir 1904-1989 (piano)
James Harry 1916-1983 (trumpet)
Kipnis Igor 1930- (harpsichord)
Landowska Wanda 1879-1959 (piano)
Levant Oscar 1906-1972 (piano)
Lhevinne Josef 1874-1944 (piano)
Menuhin Yehudi 1916-1999 (violin)
Milstein Nathan 1904-1992 (violin)
Oistraikh David 1908-1974 (violin)
Piatigorsky Gregor 1903-1976 (cello)
Rose Leonard 1918-84 (cello)
Rubinstein Anton 1829-1894 (piano)
Rubinstein Arthur 1887-1982 (piano)
Schnabel Artur 1882-1951 (piano)
Serkin Rudolf 1903-1991 (piano)
Stern Isaac 1920-2001(violin)
Tureck Roslyn 1914 - (piano)
Zuckerman Pinchas 1948 (violin)

CONDUCTORS

Barenboim Daniel 1942-
Bernstein Leonard 1918-1990
Dorati Antal 1906-1988
Fiedler Arthur 1894-1979
Foss Lucas 1922-
Klemperer Otto 1885-1973
Kostelanetz André 1901-1980
Koussevitzky Serge 1874-1951
Leinsdorf Erich 1912-1993
Levine James 1943-
Monteux Pierre 1875-1964
Ormandy Eugene 1899-1985
Previn André 1929-
Reiner Fritz 1888-1963
Rodzinski Artur 1892-1958
Solti Georg 1912-1997
Steinberg William 1899-1978
Szell George 1897-1970
Tilson Thomas Michael 1944-
Wallenstein Alfred 1898-1983
Walter Bruno 1876-1962
Whiteman Paul (1890-1967)

VOCALISTS

Kipnis Alexander 1891-1978
Merril Robert 1919-
Peters Roberta 1930-
Raisa Rosa 1893-1963
Resnik Regina 1922
Sills Beverly 1929-
Stevens Rise1913-
Warren Leonard 1911-1960

COMPOSERS

Copland Aaron 1900-1990
Dukas Paul 1865-1935
Gershwin George 1898-1937
Korngold Eric 1897-1957
Mahler Gustav 1864-1911
Meyerbeer Giacomo 1791-1864
Offenbach Jacques 1819-1880
Romberg Sigmund 1887-1951
Rubinstein Anton 1829-1894
Schoenberg, Arnold 1874-1951
Schuman William 1910-1992
Weill Kurt 1900-1950

THEATER COMPOSERS

Arlen Harold 1905-1986
Berlin Irving 1888
Blitzstein Marc 1905-1964
Gould Morton 1913-
Kern Jerome 1885-1945

Loesser Frank 1920-1969
Loewe Frederick 1901-
Rodgers Richard 1902-1979
Sondheim Stephen1930-
Styne Julie 1905

ENTERTAINERS

Bachrach Burt 1928
Bikel Theodore 1924
Brice Fanny 1891-1951
Cantor Eddie 1892-1964
Davis Jr. Sammy 1925
Dylan Bob 1941-
Garfunkel Art 1941-
Jolson Al 1886-1950
Kaye Danny 1913-
Midler Bette 1945
Miller Mitch 1911-
Shaw Artie 1910-
Shore Dinah 1917-
Simon Paul 1941-
Streisand Barbra 1942-
Tucker Sophie 1884-1966

A BASIC JEWISH MUSIC LIBRARY

The following is a partial listing of books and recordings that is representative of the panorama of Jewish music including: Israeli, Yiddish, Cantorial, Liturgical, Hassidic, Sephardic, Sabbath & Holidays, Contemporary, Children's music and Instrumental.

MUSIC BOOKS

THE INTERNATIONAL JEWISH SONGBOOK *Velvel Pasternak*
178 selections in six categories: Songs of Israel, Songs in Yiddish, Sephardic and Ladino, Sabbath and Holidays, Hassidic and Liturgical. Melody line, guitar chords, Hebrew texts, transliterations, capsule translations, annotations, discography, first line index. Hardbound .

THE JEWISH FAKE BOOK- *Velvel Pasternak*
212 songs for every possible occasion. Includes music for Weddings, Holidays, Klezmer, Israeli, Yiddish, Hasidic, Sephardic, Holidays. Melody line, chords and transliterations. categorical and alphabetical indexes

THE ULTIMATE JEWISH PIANO BOOK-
Arranged by *Edward Kalendar* and edited by *Velvel Pasternak*
111 songs for voice and piano. Popular songs in the following categories: Israel, Yiddish, Ladino, Sabbath, Festivals, Hanukah, Passover Seder, and songs in English. Includes chords, texts and transliterations

THE BEST OF ISRAELI FOLKSONGS *Velvel Pasternak*
The largest, most comprehensive collection of Israeli folksongs in print. A broad overview of songs from pre-State to present times. Melody line, chords, full Hebrew texts, transliterations, translations and annotations

JERUSALEM IN SONG- *Velvel Pasternak,*.
96 popular selections dedicated to the Holy City. Melody line, chords, Hebrew texts, transliterations, capsule translations and annotations. Also includes a selection of choral settings and songs with with piano accompaniment. Hardbound

THE SHLOMO CARLEBACH ANTHOLOGY-*Velvel Pasternak*, editor
The definitive collection of Shlomo's music in print. 133 selections represent his most popular songs recorded over a thirty year period. Melody line, chords, texts, transliterations and translations. Hardbound

THE BEST OF DEBBIE FRIEDMAN
Some of the most popular songs of America's famous Jewish songwriter/vocalist. Melody line, chords, texts, transliterations and translations.

THE ZMIROT ANTHOLOGY-Traditional Sabbath Songs For The Home
The definitive collection of *Z'mirot* for the entire Sabbath celebration compiled, edited and annotated by *Neil Levin* with *Velvel Pasternak*. More than 150 selections with melody line, chords, texts, transliterations, translations historical background and footnotes ,

JEWISH HOLIDAYS IN SONG- *Velvel Pasternak*
More than 100 beloved songs for the Sabbath and Festivals of the year. Songs for Hanukah, the *Seder*, High Holidays, *Sukot*, *Simchat Torah*, *Shavu'ot* etc. Melody line, chords, texts and transliterations ₍

THE HASIDIC ANTHOLOGY-*Velvel Pasternak*.
A revised collection of *Songs of the Chassidim Vols. I and II*. Melody line, chords, and some part-song arrangements. Topical categories include: Sabbath, High Holidays, Festivals, Passover *Seder*, Weddings, *Nigunim* and *Rikudim*. Historical introduction. annotations, Hebrew texts, transliterations and translations .

MAZEL TOV!- edited *Velvel Pasternak*
49 selections of popular traditional and contemporary melodies for weddings, Bar Mitzvahs and other joyous occasions. Includes processionals, recessionals, dinner music, Horas and Klezmer melodies for dancing

THE KLEZMER WEDDING BOOK-*Giora Feidman*
Music scored for 3 C instruments with a Bflat transposition. 17 selections suitable for any joyous occasion. Includes: Israeli, Hassidic, and Klezmer melodies

THE COMPLEAT KLEZMER-*Henry Sapoznik*
The definitive Klezmer anthology. 33 famous melodies. In depth musical analysis, discography, historical background, annotations, resources, bibliography etc.

THE NEW CHILDREN'S SONGBOOK- edited by *Velvel Pasternak*
A collection of 110 selections with melody line, chords. Jewish holiday music and folksongs suitable for young children. Includes, Hebrew texts, singable English settings. Hebrew transliterations, and activity aids.

THE GOLDEN AGE OF CANTORS-edited by *Noah Schall & Velvel Pasternak*
An overview of the greatest period of cantorial artistry. 26 cantors each represented by an acclaimed recitative, meticulously transcribed. Includes: introduction, historical overview, biographical sketches and stylistic analysis, cantorial photos and memorabilia.

SEPHARDIC/ORIENTAL SONGBOOK- edited by *Velvel Pasternak*
Songs from the liturgy, *Z'mirot*, Festivals, Ladino and folk repertoire. Melody line, chords, texts, transliterations and translations.

SEPHARDIC SONGS FOR ALL - *Ramon Tasat*
Sephardic liturgical songs and Ladino ballads from Holland, Italy, Spain. Iraq, Turkey, Morocco and Greece. Melody line, chords and texts. Guidelines for Ladino pronunciation. Companion CD enclosed.

THE NICO CASTEL LADINO SONGBOOK
35 Judeo-Spanish songs and ballads in settings for voice, piano, guitar and flute from the rep[ertoire of the noted Metropolitan Opera tenor. Includes chords, texts, pronunciation guide, translations and historical background.

THE FLORY JAGODA SONGBOOK
Flory Jagoda is acknowledged as the direct transmitter of the Bosnian Ladino musical tradition. All selections appear with melody line, chords, texts, transliterations, annotations, analysis, historical and background information.

SEPHARDIC SONGS OF PRAISE-*Abraham Cardozo*
68 melodies from the Spanish Portuguese tradition. Music for the synagogue, table songs, Festivals, High Holidays and special occasions. Melody line, chords, texts, transliterations and translations.

THE BIG KLEZMER FAKE BOOK More than 175 tunes culled from ten Tara music editions. Includes: Freylachs, Shers, Doinas, Serbas, traditional Jewish wedding dances Yiddish and Hassidic selections. Melody line, chords, transliterations, bibliography and discography

SEPHARDIC SONGS in Judeo Spanish-*Judy Frankel*
From the repertoire of the internationally acclaimed artist/lecturer. Fifty traditional and original Sephardic songs. Melody line, chords, transliterations, translations and annotations. A companion CD featuring 17 songs is included.

RECORDINGS

ISRAEL WORLD BEAT   The pulse of the Holy Land. Israeli standards with a dynamic world beat sound

THE VERY BEST OF ISRAEL Favorite Israeli folksongs performed by popular artists

MOST BEAUTIFUL JEWISH SONGS   Popular and traditional songs performed by an award-winning young women's choir

INTERNATIONAL JEWISH SONGS   Popular Jewish songs of the 20th century. Israeli, Yiddish, Sephardic, Ladino, Hassidic Sabbath, Holidays and more

MOST BEAUTIFUL SONGS OF JERUSALEM   21 selections in a many faceted tribute to the Holy City performed by outstanding artists and groups

THE GOLDEN AGE OF CANTORS   Rosenblatt, Koussevitsky, Kwartin, Hirshman and more .

TEN GREAT CANTORS   Chagy, Shlisky, Sirota, Roitman and more

GREAT VOICES OF THE SYNAGOGUE Pinchick, Roitman, Kwartin and more

IN THE FIDDLER'S HOUSE   Itzhak Perlman and four outstanding American Klezmer bands

THE KLEZMER VIOLIN   A vituoso tour de force! Classic klezmer & Hassidic melodies

KLASSIC KLEZMER-GIORA FEIDMAN   Premiere klezmer clarinetist in the world.

MAZEL TOV   Instrumental music fror a Jewish wedding, Bar Mitzvah & other joyous occasions.

JEWISH SUPER PARTY   Instrumental music suitable for parties and simchas.

THE ZMIROT ṢING-ALONG   A practical sing-along for Shabbat at home, in the synagogue, school, camp or youth group.

TGIS-THANK GOD IT'S SHABBAT   Melodies for an engaging, participatory spirited and spiritual Sabbath service.

CELEBRATE SHABBAT   Sabbath selections by outstanding, popular, contemporary artists.

SHABBOS WITH SHLOMO   A basic collection of Shlomo's popular songs for the Sabbath.

SONGS OF THE LUBAVITCHER CHASSIDIM   A classic re-issue. Redigitized and remastered CD of the first Lubvatcher recording

SONGS OF THE BOBOVER CHASSIDIM   A classic re-issue. Redigitized and remastered CD of the first two Bobover recordings.

A TREASURY OF CHASSIDIC SONG   A classic re-issue. A redigitized and re-mastered CD of the original *Od Yishoma-A Treasury of Chassidic Song* recording

SEPHARDIC SUPER PARTY   Selections of traditional Sephardic songs performed by soloist, choruses and orchestras.

GLOSSARY OF FOREIGN TERMS

Aliya—Immigration period in Israel

Ashkenaz, Ashkenazim—Jews of European extraction

Baal Shem Tov—Founder of the Hasidic Movement

Baal T'filoh—leader of a prayer service

Badchen—Wedding entertainer

Chabad—Lubavitch

Chazan— The professional precentor of the synagogue.

Chosidl—Dance (Hasidic style)

Doina— Musical composition (Rumanian in origin)

El Odon—Sabbath morning prayer recited in the *Shacharit* service

Farbrengen— Hasidic gatherings.

Hakofos— The ritual march of the worshippers carrying the *Toroh* Scrolls around the altar on the festival of *Simchas Toroh*

Havurot—Non-synagogal prayer groups

Hora— Circle dance

K'dusha— Prayer recited during morning synagogue services

Kabbala—Mystical teachings of Judaism

Klezmer—lit. Instrument of music, a genre of Jewish music

L'cho Dodi— Prayer recited in the Friday evening service

Magrepha—Musical instrument used during Temple times

M'gillah—Scroll e.g. *Esther, Song of Songs* etc.

Midrash—Rabbinic literature, homily, exegesis and sermons based on the Bible

Mimkomcho— Prayer in the Sabbath and Festival *Shacharit* service

Mincha— Daily afternoon service

Minhag—Custom

Mishna— The codification of the oral tradition of basic Jewish law

Misinai—emanating from Mt. Sinai

Misnagdim—Opponents of Hasidim

Mitzva, Mitzvos—Commandment, good deeds

Musaph—Additional morning service on Sabbath and holidays

Nigun, Neginah, Nigunim—Melody(ies) especially wordless tunes of the Hasidim.

Nusach Hatfila— chant patterns of the prayer service

Pentateuch—The Bible

Pesach—Passover

Piyut—Religious poetry added to certain parts of the service

Rebbe—Rabbi or teacher; a Hasidic rabbi or leader

Rikud—Dance

Rosh Hashonoh— The Jewish "New Year"

Shabbos—Sabbath

Shacharit year— The morning prayer service

Shaliach Tsibur—Leader of communal prayers

Shchino —The Divine Presence—term used in rabbinic literature

Sher—Dance (of Russian origin)

Shofar —Ram's horn used in the synagogue during the High Holidays.

Shtetl—Small town in Eastern Europe

Simchas Toroh—Festival which closes the holiday of *Sukot*.

Simcho—Joy, joyous celebration

Sukah—Temporary living abode for the holiday of *Sukot*

Sukot—Holiday of Tabernacles

T'fila—Prayer

Talmud —The Oral Law-a body of text comprising the *Mishna* and commentary and discussions on it

Tfilin—Phylacteries

Torah, Toroh—The Bible

Tsadik, Tsadikim— Righteous or saintly being (s).

Yeshiva—Academy of Rabbinic and Talmudic learning

Yom Kippur— The "Day of Atonement."

Z'mirot —Domestic Sabbath songs chanted in the home.

Zohar —The title of the fundamental book of the *Kabbala*